Genetically
Modified Food

WITHDRAWN

Other Books of Related Interest:

GLOBALVIEWPOINTS

Genetically Modified Food

Noël Merino, Book Editor

GREENHAVEN PRESS
A part of Gale, Cengage Learning

GALE
CENGAGE Learning·

Farmington Hills, Mich • San Francisco • New York • Waterville, Maine
Meriden, Conn • Mason, Ohio • Chicago

Elizabeth Des Chenes, *Director, Content Strategy*
Douglas Dentino, *Manager, New Product*

© 2014 Greenhaven Press, a part of Gale, Cengage Learning

WCN: 01-100-101

Gale and Greenhaven Press are registered trademarks used herein under license.

For more information, contact:
Greenhaven Press
27500 Drake Rd.
Farmington Hills, MI 48331-3535
Or you can visit our Internet site at gale.cengage.com

For product information and technology assistance, contact us at

Gale Customer Support, 1-800-877-4253
For permission to use material from this text or product, submit all requests online at
www.cengage.com/permissions

Further permissions questions can be emailed to permissionrequest@cengage.com

Articles in Greenhaven Press anthologies are often edited for length to meet page requirements. In addition, original titles of these works are changed to clearly present the main thesis and to explicitly indicate the author's opinion. Every effort is made to ensure that Greenhaven Press accurately reflects the original intent of the authors. Every effort has been made to trace the owners of copyrighted material.

Cover image © Jim Richardson/Corbis.

LIBRARY OF CONGRESS CATALOGING-IN-PUBLICATION DATA

Genetically modified food / Noël Merino, book editor.
      pages cm. -- (Global viewpoints)
      Includes bibliographical references and index.
      ISBN 978-0-7377-6910-4 (hardcover) -- ISBN 978-0-7377-6911-1 (pbk.)
      1. Genetically modified foods. 2. Food--Biotechnology. I. Merino, Noël. II. Series:
      Global viewpoints.
      TP248.65.F6645747 2014
      664--dc23

                                                                              2014000928

Printed in the United States of America
1 2 3 4 5 6 7 18 17 16 15 14

Contents

Chapter 2: The Impact of Genetically Modified Crops on Agriculture

Studies show that the promised increased yields from genetic modification have not materialized and that the biotechnology has actually decreased yields in some cases.

Chapter 3: The Impact of Genetically Modified Food on Health

Chapter 4: Regulations Regarding Genetically Modified Food

Foreword

*"The problems of all of humanity can
only be solved by all of humanity."*
—*Swiss author Friedrich Dürrenmatt*

Global interdependence has become an undeniable reality. Mass media and technology have increased worldwide access to information and created a society of global citizens. Understanding and navigating this global community is a challenge, requiring a high degree of information literacy and a new level of learning sophistication.

Building on the success of its flagship series, Opposing Viewpoints, Greenhaven Press has created the Global Viewpoints series to examine a broad range of current, often controversial topics of worldwide importance from a variety of international perspectives. Providing students and other readers with the information they need to explore global connections and think critically about worldwide implications, each Global Viewpoints volume offers a panoramic view of a topic of widespread significance.

Drugs, famine, immigration—a broad, international treatment is essential to do justice to social, environmental, health, and political issues such as these. Junior high, high school, and early college students, as well as general readers, can all use Global Viewpoints anthologies to discern the complexities relating to each issue. Readers will be able to examine unique national perspectives while, at the same time, appreciating the interconnectedness that global priorities bring to all nations and cultures.

Material in each volume is selected from a diverse range of sources, including journals, magazines, newspapers, nonfiction books, speeches, government documents, pamphlets, organization newsletters, and position papers. Global Viewpoints is truly global, with material drawn primarily from international sources available in English and secondarily from US sources with extensive international coverage.

Features of each volume in the Global Viewpoints series include:

- An **annotated table of contents** that provides a brief summary of each essay in the volume, including the name of the country or area covered in the essay.

- An **introduction** specific to the volume topic.

- A **world map** to help readers locate the countries or areas covered in the essays.

- For each viewpoint, an **introduction** that contains notes about the author and source of the viewpoint explains why material from the specific country is being presented, summarizes the main points of the viewpoint, and offers three **guided reading questions** to aid in understanding and comprehension.

- **For further discussion** questions that promote critical thinking by asking the reader to compare and contrast aspects of the viewpoints or draw conclusions about perspectives and arguments.

- A worldwide list of **organizations to contact** for readers seeking additional information.

- A **periodical bibliography** for each chapter and a **bibliography of books** on the volume topic to aid in further research.

- A comprehensive **subject index** to offer access to people, places, events, and subjects cited in the text, with the countries covered in the viewpoints highlighted.

Global Viewpoints is designed for a broad spectrum of readers who want to learn more about current events, history, political science, government, international relations, economics, environmental science, world cultures, and sociology—students doing research for class assignments or debates, teachers and faculty seeking to supplement course materials, and others wanting to understand current issues better. By presenting how people in various countries perceive the root causes, current consequences, and proposed solutions to worldwide challenges, Global Viewpoints volumes offer readers opportunities to enhance their global awareness and their knowledge of cultures worldwide.

Introduction

> *"The release of GMOs [genetically modified organisms] into the environment and the marketing of GM [genetically modified] foods have resulted in a public debate in many parts of the world."*
>
> —*World Health Organization (WHO), "20 Questions on Genetically Modified Foods"*

The genetic modification of food is the process of deliberately modifying genes, a type of agricultural biotechnology also known as genetic engineering. The modification of genes entails manipulating the DNA, or deoxyribonucleic acid, of organisms at the molecular level using recombinant DNA techniques; that is, techniques that recombine genes. Enzymes are used to remove or add pieces of DNA—altering, adding, or deleting genes. Frequently the genes from one organism are removed and inserted into another organism. Food that is the result of genetic engineering is becoming common throughout the world, although attitudes about and regulation of this biotechnology vary widely.

The first genetically engineered crop to be approved commercially was the Flavr Savr tomato, approved by the US Food and Drug Administration (FDA) in 1994. The Flavr Savr tomato was developed by combining the genes of a tomato with the *E. coli* bacterium in order to delay the softening and rotting of the tomato. The resulting Flavr Savr tomatoes did not succeed on the commercial market, and production ended a few years later. However, several genetically modified food crops gained regulatory approval and commercial success beginning in the mid-1990s, with primary growth occurring for genetically modified soybeans, corn (or maize), and canola (or rapeseed).

According to the US Department of Agriculture, 93 percent of soybeans and 90 percent of corn in the United States were genetically modified as of 2013. Although this widespread growth and acceptance of genetically modified crops is not present worldwide, in recent years growth of genetically modified crops has expanded worldwide. According to the International Service for the Acquisition of Agri-Biotech Applications (ISAAA), hectarage—or acreage—of biotech crops has increased every single year from 1996 to 2012. In 2012 the top biotech food crops in order of hectarage were soybean, maize, and canola. Other genetically modified food crops cultivated include alfalfa, sugar beet, papaya, squash, tomato, and sweet pepper. ISAAA notes that in 2012, for the first time, developing countries grew more genetically modified crops than industrial countries. Although the United States is the leading producer of genetically modified crops in the world, it is followed by Brazil, Argentina, India, and Canada.

Whereas the growth of genetically modified crops has been increasing in North America, South America, and Asia over the past couple decades, growth in Europe and Africa has been less notable. In Europe, the lack of genetically modified crops can be explained by the lack of approval of many genetically modified crops for growth and, in some instances, outright bans on the production and sale of genetically modified food. Although the European Commission—the executive body of the European Union—approved the cultivation of genetically modified corn in 1997, several countries in the European Union have since decided to ban the production of genetically modified corn, including France, Germany, Greece, Austria, Luxembourg, and Hungary. In Switzerland, there is a moratorium on the production of all genetically modified organisms through 2017. Nonetheless, several other countries in Europe do grow genetically modified corn, with Spain as the largest producer.

Africa has been resistant to the adoption of genetically modified crops, and as of 2013 only four African countries—Burkina Faso, Egypt, Sudan, and South Africa—have fully commercialized genetically modified crops. In several countries—including Angola, Ethiopia, Kenya, Lesotho, Madagascar, Malawi, Mozambique, Swaziland, Tanzania, Zambia, and Zimbabwe—even the import of genetically modified food is banned unless the food is fully milled, thus preventing genetically modified seeds from spreading to local crops.

Genetic modification has not been limited to plants that are eaten for food. At the present time, no genetically modified animals are in the food supply anywhere in the world. However, there are ongoing developments to bring genetically modified salmon to the marketplace: AquAdvantage salmon is currently under consideration by the FDA. Elsewhere, there has been an attempt to develop genetically modified pigs: Canada abandoned its development of the so-called Enviropig in 2012 for lack of funding.

Beyond the genetic modification of animals for direct consumption, however, genetic modification has also been used in the development of hormones given to dairy cattle. In the 1980s the gene for bovine somatotropin—a cow hormone that regulates milk production—was cloned and injected into the *E. coli* bacterium. The resulting hormone—recombinant bovine somatotropin (rBST), also known as recombinant bovine growth hormone (rBGH)—is harvested and purified, and then injected into dairy cows to increase milk production. The FDA approved rBST in 1993, and many dairy farmers began using the genetically engineered growth hormone. The use of rBST is banned in Canada, all countries of the European Union, Japan, Australia, and New Zealand. Among the reasons for the ban in these countries are concerns about animal welfare and concerns about human health.

Genetically modified food is becoming more widespread every year, but there is by no means worldwide acceptance of the biotechnology. Even in countries that have widespread growth of genetically modified crops, controversies abound about the safety of the resulting food. In the United States and elsewhere, consumer groups argue for better labeling and information about what foods contain genetically modified ingredients, safety issues aside. The various global attitudes toward the benefits and safety of genetically modified foods, as well as the different approaches to regulation of such foods, are explored in *Global Viewpoints: Genetically Modified Food*, shedding light on this timely social controversy.

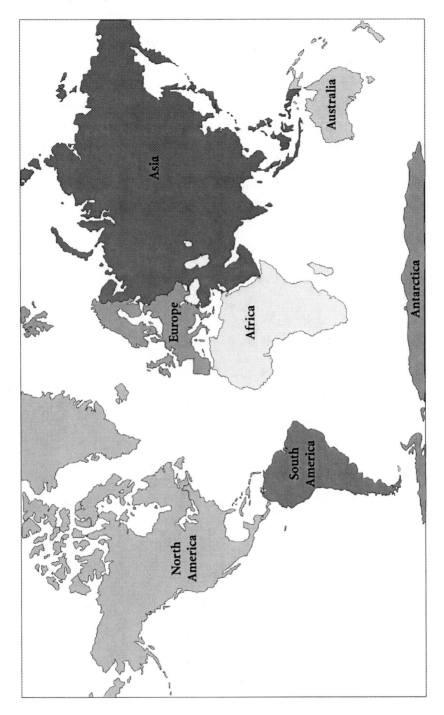

Attitudes Toward Genetically Modified Food Around the World

In the United States, Genetically Modified Food Is Common

Gregory Jaffe

In the following viewpoint, Gregory Jaffe argues that genetically engineered crops are commonly grown and present in most processed foods. Jaffe contends that the biotechnology of genetically engineering plants or animals is not that different from classical breeding, allowing manipulation that can improve crops. Jaffe claims that most corn, soybeans, and sugar beets in the United States are genetically modified and used as food for both farm animals and humans. Jaffe is director of biotechnology at the Center for Science in the Public Interest.

As you read, consider the following questions:

1. According to the author, food manufacturers estimate that what percentage of processed foods contain at least one genetically modified ingredient?

2. Jaffe claims that most of the commercial genetically engineered crops grown in the United States contain genes that serve one of what two purposes?

3. According to the author, which countries are the four largest adopters of genetically engineered crops outside of the United States?

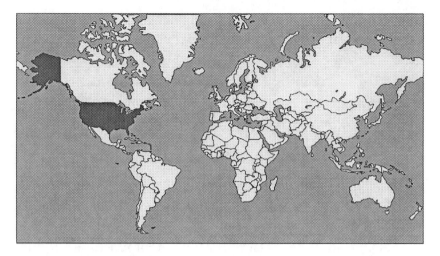

In the past 15 years, genetically engineered (GE) crops have become part of mainstream agriculture in developed and developing countries alike. American farmers planted 170 million acres of GE corn, soybeans, cotton, canola, sugar beets, alfalfa, papaya, and squash in 2011. Food manufacturers estimate that 70 percent of processed foods contain at least one ingredient made from those GE crops. Their advent, however, has not been without controversy and concern for human health and the environment, and critics, as well as devotees, are plentiful. . . .

Genetically Engineered Organisms

What does it mean to "genetically engineer" an organism?

When scientists genetically engineer a plant or animal, they remove a gene from one organism (or a specific variety of an organism) and transfer that gene to a different organism (or different variety) using recombinant DNA methods. The new gene becomes integrated into every cell of the organism and is inherited by the organism's offspring. In most cases, the new gene produces a new protein, which then provides the organism with some useful trait. In some cases, scientists use this technique to silence an existing gene (i.e., to prevent its expression) or to get a plant to express an otherwise silent gene.

American farmers planted 170 million acres of GE corn, soybeans, cotton, canola, sugar beets, alfalfa, papaya, and squash in 2011.

Is the use of genetic engineering different from classical breeding of plants and the way new plant varieties have long been developed?

Yes and no. With classical breeding, reproduction can only occur between closely related species. That means that a corn plant can only mate with another corn plant or a closely related species. Similarly, a cow can only mate with another cow. Thus, classical or conventional breeding is usually limited to the DNA variety found within a species. With genetic engineering, however, any gene from any organism can be transferred to a different organism. Thus, that allows a snippet of DNA that codes for an insecticidal protein from a bacterium, such as *Bacillus thuringiensis* (Bt), to be transferred into a corn or cotton plant.

Plant breeders, however, have long used a variety of techniques to introduce variation into the DNA of a species and obtain varieties with desirable traits. For example, scientists have used chemicals to cause DNA mutations and then selected the organisms with the desired trait. Similarly, scientists have blasted plant cells with X-rays and gamma radiation to induce mutations. Americans have eaten varieties of wheat, rice and pink grapefruits that were generated from radiation mutagenesis. So while moving single genes from one species to another in the laboratory is a relatively new agricultural breeding method, scientists have been manipulating plants in "unnatural" ways for over fifty years to create varieties that would not otherwise be found in nature.

Genetically Modified Dairy Products in the United States

RBGH, or recombinant bovine growth hormone, is a GE [genetically engineered] variation on a naturally occurring hormone injected into dairy cows to increase milk production. It is banned for milk destined for human consumption in the European Union, Canada, New Zealand, and Australia. Many milk brands that are rBGH-free label their milk as such, but as much as 40 percent of our dairy products, including ice cream and cheese, contains the hormone.

Maggie Caldwell, "5 Surprising Genetically Modified Foods,"
Mother Jones, August 5, 2013.

Genetically engineering a plant is not a panacea for addressing the agricultural constraints faced by farmers. Conventional breeding can often be used to obtain the same advantageous traits as obtained through genetic engineering, though adding a new gene through genetic engineering can often be quicker and more precise. Rather, genetic engineering should be seen as one of the many tools available for use by plant breeders to improve crop varieties so that we increase food production, control pests, and improve farm profits.

Traits Engineered into Agricultural Crops

Most of the commercial genetically engineered ("GE") crops grown in the United States contain genes that provide either resistance to pests or tolerance to herbicides. GE corn and cotton contain genes from the soil bacterium *Bacillus thuringiensis* (Bt). The proteins produced from those genes kill certain insect pests when they are ingested, eliminating the need to use chemical pesticides. Different Bt genes produce proteins that target different pests.

GE soybeans, corn, canola, sugar beets, cotton, and alfalfa contain one of several bacterial genes that protect the crop from particular herbicides. Those genes allow certain herbicides to be applied to the crop without harming it, giving farmers more flexible use of herbicides to control weeds, such as treating a field after the crop has emerged, not just before.

Finally, some varieties of squash and papaya have been engineered with plant virus genes that render those crops resistant to those plant viruses. More recently, scientists engineered plum trees to resist the plum pox virus, but those varieties have not been commercialized yet. Countless other traits—such as drought tolerance and more healthful fatty acids in soybeans and other oilseeds—have been engineered into plants in the laboratory, but also have not yet commercialized in the United States.

The Prevalence of Genetically Engineered Crops

How prevalent are genetically engineered crops in the United States?

In 2011, approximately 88% of all field corn (mostly used for cattle feed and ethanol production), 94% of all soybeans, 95% of all sugar beets, and 90% of all cotton grown in the United States were genetically engineered with one to as many as seven different genes. U.S. farmers also grew GE canola as well as small amounts of genetically engineered papayas, summer squash, and insect-resistant sweet corn. All these engineered crops totaled approximately 170 million acres in 2011.

How prevalent are genetically engineered crops outside the United States?

According to the International Service for the Acquisition of Agri-Biotech Applications (ISAAA), 16.7 million farmers in 29 countries planted over 395 million acres of biotech crops in 2011. The largest adopters outside the United States include Brazil, Argentina, India, Canada, and China. Even in Europe, where opposition to GE runs high, eight countries—Portugal, Spain, Germany, Sweden, Czech Republic, Poland, Slovakia, and Romania—had a limited number of farmers who grew either GE corn or potatoes.

Americans consume thousands of foods with ingredients derived from genetically engineered crops daily.

Am I currently eating genetically engineered foods?

Although most soybeans and field corn are genetically engineered, the harvest from those crops goes primarily to feeding cows, pigs, and chickens. Some genetically engineered corn and soybeans, however, do get used for human food products. Field corn is used to make cornmeal for products like muffins, corn chips, and tortillas. Far more field corn is used to produce high-fructose corn syrup (HFCS) which is used to sweeten soda pop and other foods, and corn oil that might be used for cooking or baking.

GE soybeans are processed to make soybean oil and soy lecithin, an emulsifier used in many foods. GE canola and cotton are also processed to produce canola oil or cotton-seed oil, both of which are used for cooking. GE sugar beets are used to produce sugar, which can be found in many foods. Therefore, countless processed foods contain ingredients that were derived from GE corn, soybeans, canola, sugar beets, or cotton.

Although products such as soy oil, beet sugar, and fructose sweeteners were produced from GE crops, the process of producing the oil, sugar, and HFCS from the crop eliminates virtually all of the transgene and its protein product. So although Americans consume thousands of foods with ingredients derived from genetically engineered crops daily, our diets actually expose us to very little of the engineered gene or their protein products.

In South America, Genetically Modified Crops Are Rapidly Expanding

Friends of the Earth International

In the following viewpoint, Friends of the Earth International argues that there has been a rapid advance in the cultivation of genetically modified crops in the South American Southern Cone countries of Brazil, Argentina, Paraguay, Uruguay, and Chile, with negative impacts. The author claims that much of the increased cultivation is unauthorized, although new genetically modified crops have been approved. Friends of the Earth International is a grassroots environmental network that unites more than seventy national organizations with thousands of local groups.

As you read, consider the following questions:

1. According to the author, in Uruguay what social concern has resulted from the expansion of soy agribusiness?

2. What percentage of soy grown in Argentina in the 2008–2009 season was genetically modified?

3. According to Friends of the Earth International, how many new genetically modified varieties were approved in 2009 in the Southern Cone?

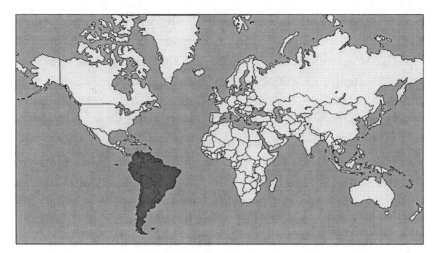

The Southern Cone of [South] America is a region of prime importance for global food production, and has been specifically targeted by transnational agribusiness for the commercial production of GM [genetically modified] crops. Along with the US, the Southern Cone is now responsible for more than 80% of the total area planted with GMOs [genetically modified organisms] worldwide.

The Social and Environmental Impacts

Genetically modified organisms are now a key element of agribusiness development, particularly in this region. Technological 'packages' have been developed, based on the use of agricultural machinery and genetically modified seeds and biocides, which enable a quick return on invested capital. These packages require little manual labor and externalize associated environmental and social costs. As a result, agribusiness has become particularly attractive to investors and speculative capital. In recent years there has been a significant flow of capital from various financial sectors towards GM agriculture.

However, the rapid advance of agribusiness and genetic engineering in the Southern Cone has brought with it serious social and environmental impacts that are not being adequately dealt with by governments. Booming agribusiness is displacing peasant and indigenous communities; pushing the agricultural frontier deeper into the forests; increasing pollution and health problems because of the increased use of biocides; accelerating the erosion of natural resources; and destroying peoples' knowledge and food sovereignty.

As a result of all this, farmers and social organizations are actively resisting the advance of agribusiness. In particular, soy has seen spectacular growth in the last decade, and battles over soy expansion illustrate the social tensions created by the rapid concentration of land, wealth and power. In Paraguay, for example, displacements and the indiscriminate use of herbicides on soy plantations have led to serious conflicts and the murder of Paraguayan peasants. In Brazil, a demonstration organized by the landless workers' movement, Movimento dos Trabalhadores Rurais sem Terra (MST), against an experimental area managed by Syngenta, ended with a peasant being shot dead by security guards hired by the company. In Uruguay, the expansion of soy agribusiness has displaced family agriculture, because the increase in agribusiness has increased land rental rates; and thus the main organization of family farmers (Comisión Nacional de Fomento Rural) has asked the Uruguayan government to limit the expansion of agribusiness in order to prevent the complete disappearance of family farming.

The rapid advance of agribusiness and genetic engineering in the Southern Cone has brought with it serious social and environmental impacts.

Agribusiness interests in the region also exert considerable influence and can be difficult for governments to resist. In Bolivia, for example, one of the main leaders of the Media Luna (the richest region of the country), and president of the Pro-Santa Cruz Civic Committee, Branko Marinkovic, is also one of the main soy producers in the region. This committee promoted the creation of an autonomist movement in defense of the interests of the powerful local elite and opposed to recognizing the rights of the original peoples. This posed a serious problem for the administration of Bolivian president Evo Morales, and several indigenous people were murdered as a consequence of this conflict.

Similarly there was a sharp conflict between the 'campo' (the countryside) and the Argentinean government in 2008, when soy industrialists opposed the government's restrictions on commodity exports.

The Advance of Genetically Modified Crops

At present, GM crops occupy around 37 million ha [hectares] in the Southern Cone, which represents one-third of the surface area dedicated to GM crops around the world. The main GM crop is soy, but GM maize and cotton are also being cultivated. Apart from the United States, Argentina and Brazil are the world's two main producers of GM crops. Within the region, Argentina has the largest surface area of GM crops (19 million ha), followed by Brazil (with 14.5 million ha).

Agribusiness's intense drive to find countries willing to cultivate genetically engineered crops on a commercial scale has given a new momentum to the expansion of intensive industrial agriculture in the Southern Cone region, undoing much that had previously been done to develop agri-ecological farming in the area. This is most marked in terms of the expansion of GM soy.

In the season 2008/2009 some 21.7 million ha of soybeans were sown in Brazil, and for 2009/2010 around 23 million ha of soy are expected to be sown, generating a record crop of 64 million tons. According to estimates from the private sector, around 60% of the area (around 13 million ha) is genetically modified Roundup Ready (RR) soy.

In Argentina, soy crops covered around 18 million ha (equivalent to more than 75% of the area occupied by summer crops) but as a result of the drought of the summer 2008/2009, only 16.8 million were harvested. Almost 100% of this was RR soy.

Apart from the United States, Argentina and Brazil are the world's two main producers of GM crops.

In Paraguay, according to the National Agricultural Survey (CNA, using its Spanish acronym), 2.5 million ha of soy were sown in 2008/2009 (nearly 60% of the total agricultural area of the country) of which 80% was RR soy.

In Uruguay, soy occupied 580,000 ha in the season 2008/2009 representing 75% of the surface sown with summer crops, and nearly 100% of this was RR soy. In Bolivia, 50% of the agricultural land (around 940,000 ha) was sown with soy in 2009; and 70% of this, according to ANAPO [Oilseed and Wheat Producers Association], was RR soy.

As a whole, soy crops in the region occupied 42.5 million ha (425,000 km^2), of which 33 million were RR soy; the overall production of soybean was 97 million tons.

In relation to corn, some 14 million ha were sown in Brazil in the 2008/2009 season. The Council of Information on Biotechnology (CIB), an organization that promotes GM technology in Brazil, estimates that 1.3 million ha of this was GM corn. In Argentina, for the same season, nearly 3.5 million ha was sown with corn, although only 2.3 million was actually harvested due to drought. Of this, 83% was GM corn, according to ArgenBio, an organization that brings together GM seed multinationals operating in Argentina. In Uruguay, although there is no data for the total area sown with GM corn, 82% of the seed imported in 2008 was GM. It is thus possible to calculate that around 80% of the area cultivated in Uruguay in the 2008/2009 season (over a total sown area of 87,500 ha) was planted with GM corn.

Surface Area of GM Crops in Thousands of HA (2008–2009)

Country	Soy	Corn	Cotton	Canola/ oilseed rape	Total
Argentina	16,800.0	1,910.0	280	–	18,990.0
Brazil	13,000.0	1,300.0	250	–	14,550.0
Paraguay	2,000.0	–	–	–	2,000.0
Uruguay	580.0	72.0	–	–	652.0
Bolivia	650.0	–	–	–	650.0
Chile*	0.2	11.6	–	4.1	15.9

The data for this table was collected from several sources because there is no official data available corresponding to each country. Argentina: MAGyP Argentina, ArgenBio; Brazil: CONAB, Report from an EU mission in Brazil, RPC, CIB; Paraguay: MAG; Uruguay: MGAP; Bolivia: ANAPO; Chile: SAG.
* For Chile the data relates to surface dedicated to seed plots.

TAKEN FROM: Friends of the Earth International, "GMOs in the Southern Cone," *Who Benefits from GM Crops? The Great Climate Change Swindle*, issue 117, September 2010.

For cotton, Brazil planted 840,000 ha in 2008/2009, of which 250,000 ha was GM cotton according to CIB. In Argentina, 94% of the total of almost 300,000 ha of cotton was sown with GM seeds.

In Chile, GM seeds are only allowed to be used for the production of seeds for export (at present they are discussing a future biosafety law and whether or not they should authorize the commercial release of GMOs). The main GM crop grown is corn, at 11,850 ha, followed by canola at 4,054 ha, and soy at 204 ha.

The Unauthorized Growth of GM Crops

In the Southern Cone, the introduction of genetically modified crops started in 1996, when Argentina and Uruguay authorized the cultivation of Monsanto RR soy. Neither country conducted an environmental impact study, and no assessments were made of the likely social and economic impacts.

GM soy was then transferred illegally from Argentina and Uruguay, into Brazil, Paraguay and Bolivia. Seed companies subsequently chose to develop and promote their products in these countries on the basis of a *fait accompli* strategy—it is already there, and it is unalterable. In Brazil, two other Monsanto GM products, Bollgard cotton and GA21 corn also entered the country illegally (in 2004 and 2005 respectively).

In Paraguay, the NGO [nongovernmental organization] Alter Vida estimates that around 8,000 ha are currently being cultivated with GM cotton, even though the approval process has not passed the evaluation stage yet. Similarly, most of the GM cotton sown in Argentina seems to be a cultivar with two stacked GM traits that has not yet been authorized for planting. The governments have responded to this strategy with a policy that essentially enshrines impunity. Instead of issuing and enforcing sanctions to control the illegal introduction of these crops in their countries, they have adapted their country's regulations to allow for GM crops. In Brazil they have even used the fact that they are already being grown as an argument for authorizing GM crops.

In the Southern Cone, the introduction of genetically modified crops started in 1996.

The Approval of GM Crops

During 2009, several new GM varieties were approved in the region. Three GM varieties of cotton, five of corn and one of soy were released in Brazil. The latter is the first GM variety released that was also developed in Brazil, as a result of an agreement between BASF and Embrapa Soja (a part-public Brazilian firm dedicated to agricultural research). This GM variety is tolerant to herbicides of the imidazolinone group and is presented as an alternative to RR soy to fight those weeds that have already developed a resistance to glyphosate.

In Argentina, a new GM cotton variety has also been released and several licenses have been granted to produce GM corn seeds for export (even though these do not yet have a commercial release approval) on the condition that they have been approved at the destination country. In 2008 (no update is available for 2009), 49 licenses were granted to produce GM corn seeds, including 13 to Monsanto and 8 to Syngenta. 180 experimental releases were also authorized including for soy, maize, wheat, sugar cane, cotton, rice, safflower, orange, potato and alfalfa.

In Uruguay, after lifting the moratorium on new GM releases (in place from January 2007 to July 2008), the evaluation of five new GM traits in maize was approved; and the production of two new types of GM soy was also authorized, although only for export (which conveniently allows producers to skip the two-year evaluation process required for any GM crop to be commercially released within the country).

All new GM releases consist of GM traits related to herbicide tolerance (glyphosate or glufosinate ammonium) and/or lepidoptera resistance, either individually or stacked together.

Food: Rumpus over GM Food Aid

IRIN (Integrated Regional Information Networks)

In the following viewpoint, IRIN (Integrated Regional Information Networks) contends that there is controversy in Africa about allowing genetically modified organisms in food. The author claims that several African countries have banned or placed conditions on the acceptance of food that is genetically modified. The author argues that the conflicting policies on genetically modified food in the United States and Europe have created mistrust regarding the technology. IRIN is a news agency of the United Nations Office for the Coordination of Humanitarian Affairs focusing on humanitarian stories.

As you read, consider the following questions:

1. According to the author, which African country in 2002 said it would not accept genetically modified food aid in any form?

2. Which European countries have banned the cultivation of all genetically modified organisms, according to the author?

3. According to the African Biosafety Network of Expertise (ABNE), what are the only three African countries commercially producing genetically modified crops?

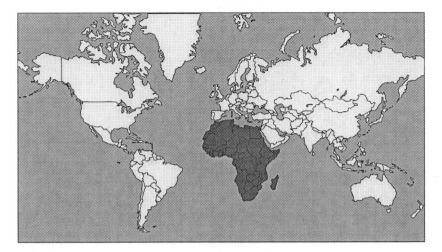

Genetically modified (GM) food aid bound for Africa has long been a bone of contention among governments, scientists, activists, consumers and aid workers.

On 18 August a drought-affected Kenyan government fired the head of its National Biosafety Authority for expediting the process to import milled food aid which might have contained genetically modified organisms (GMO). In the weeks preceding and after the incident, public debate on the issue was distorted by extreme positions either for or against GM food.

"When you have people starving in your country you don't simply turn your back on food at your doorstep just because it is labelled GM—it is expected that biosafety risk assessments should have been conducted before the importation of the food to see whether it does indeed pose a threat before taking a decision. Taking this decision so late in the day could have serious consequences for the suffering people," says Diran Makinde, director of the New Partnership for Africa's Development's (NEPAD's) African Biosafety Network of Expertise (ABNE), a pool of scientific experts set up by the African Union.

There have been different degrees of resistance to GM food and GM food aid in Africa.

In 2002 Zambia announced it would not accept GM food aid in any form. Positions were polarized to a great extent after a quote from a US State Department official, "Beggars can't be choosers", hit the headlines. It prompted the then president, Levy Mwanawasa, to say hunger was no reason for feeding his people "poison". Since then Zambia has become a poster child for the anti-GM lobby.

Zimbabwe, Malawi and Mozambique said they could allow imports of GM food aid in its milled form as this eliminated the risk of the germination of whole grains and limited possible contamination of local varieties.

There have been different degrees of resistance to GM food and GM food aid in Africa.

Lesotho and Swaziland allowed the distribution of non-milled GM food/grains, but warned people that it was for consumption, not cultivation.

In 2004, Angola and Sudan announced restrictions on GM food aid.

Cautious Approach

Most African countries approach GM technology applied to crops with caution.

"Why shouldn't we be wary of this technology and its possible long-term health impacts, if the EU [European Union] is? If it is not good for them, why should it be good for us?" said Tewolde Egziabher, Ethiopia's director of the Environmental Protection Authority.

Egziabher was one of the main architects of the Cartagena Protocol, the international law on biosafety which came into effect in 2003 and which allows countries to impose bans on foods containing GM.

The protocol's cornerstone is "precaution", notes a UN Environment Programme briefing. It gives governments the discretion to impose bans even where there is insufficient scientific evidence about the potential adverse effects of GM crops. The USA has yet to ratify the protocol.

GM technology injects foreign genes into a crop that can improve its appearance, taste, nutritional quality, drought tolerance, and insect and disease resistance. There has been cautious optimism about the new technology in some quarters.

"As crop yields drop because of weather shocks, GM technology is not the panacea, as Africa will feel the impact of climate change in the long term. But it is potentially yet another tool in our fight to improve production," said Per Pinstrup-Andersen, 2001 World Food Prize laureate and the author of a book on the politics of GM food.

Most critics of GM food, however, argue that foreign genes can produce toxic proteins and allergens, even possibly transfer the genes to bacteria in the human gut; or transfer these traits to other crops with unknown consequences.

Global Divide

A deep mistrust also prevails in Africa, given the fact that two power blocs—the EU and the USA—remain divided over GM.

Only one strain of GM maize, Monsanto 810, and one modified potato, have been approved in the EU, and most countries grow neither commercially. Spain accounts for about 80 percent of GMO grown in the EU in terms of land under cultivation, but Austria, France, Greece, Hungary, Germany and Luxembourg have banned all GMO cultivation.

On the other hand, in the USA, where 70 percent of maize is GM, GM food need not be labelled. Some food experts say both the EU and the USA have vested interests in promoting

African Model Law on Biosafety

ARTICLE 19: COMMUNITY RIGHTS FOR
GM FREE ZONES

   Taking into account the provisions of Article 26 of the Cartagena Protocol on Biosafety and the provisions of the Convention on Biological Diversity on the conservation and sustainable utilization of biological diversity:

1. The Competent Authority shall develop policies that protect the rights of communities to declare GMO [genetically modified organism] free zones.

2. The Competent Authority shall take measures for the creation of geographical areas that are declared as 'GMO free zones' where the release of any GMO is prohibited.

"Draft Revised African Model Law on Biosafety," January 2008.

their respective views in Africa, which is seen as a potential market and supplier of either GM or non-GM products.

A deep mistrust ... prevails in Africa, given the fact that two power blocs—the EU and the USA—remain divided over GM.

In Africa, the production of GM food is still in its infancy. South Africa (70–80 percent of its maize, soya and cotton production), Egypt (maize) and Burkina Faso (cotton) are the only African countries commercially producing GM crops, according to ABNE.

Traditionally the USA has been the biggest donor in kind to the World Food Programme (WFP). But the aid agency is trying to broaden its source of food aid. In 2010, WFP said 36 percent of its food aid, or two million out of 5.7 million tons disbursed globally, was procured in developing countries.

While wheat accounts for more than 50 percent of WFP's global cereal component, GM wheat does not figure as it is not grown commercially. According to data from 2006, at least 38 percent of cereal food aid to Africa was wheat and wheat flour, said Christopher Barrett, a food aid expert. Though wheat tends to be a less important part of the African diet than maize, aid agencies sometimes offer wheat instead of GM maize in emergencies.

Possible Solutions

Milling the grain is an obvious solution, said Julia Steets, an aid policy expert at the Global Public Policy Institute. "Milling either at source or in the port of arrival or in the prepositioning warehouses—it would of course also help to know in advance which governments take what positions on that, so that the food aid agencies are prepared."

The stance of recipient countries has to be respected. When a country prohibits GMO, sourcing alternative commodities and routes can "obviously impact delivery times and costs but those are the parameters in which we work," said David Orr, WFP spokesman. "We always abide by the laws and regulations of recipient countries."

If a country is not receptive to GM food—"give the country the money for procurement of the food from an African country with a surplus (local procurement is better than shipping food all the way from the US anyway)," said Pinstrup-Andersen.

Food aid agencies in Africa usually turn to South Africa for surplus maize. The country has systems in place to segregate non-GM from GM, says Thom Jayne, professor of international development at Michigan State University.

Farmers in South Africa certify non-GM content by conducting a basic test, which detects specific proteins produced by a GM plant. The non-GM grain is separated from the rest before being shipped.

The stance of recipient countries has to be respected.

Another way of separating GM from non-GM crops involves contract-farming schemes first set up in 2004–2005. The process involves the purchaser identifying farmers who buy non-GM seed. Tests are conducted on their field for any traces of GM before they are offered a contract.

But all these measures involve extra costs.

Legislation

In 2001 the African Union drafted the African Model Law on Biosafety but taking an even more cautious approach than the protocol, allowing countries to adopt more stringent measures to assess the safety of GM food.

National biosafety laws exist in 17 of the 54 African countries. In most countries, the legislation is a work in progress.

Labelling and verifying the content of a crop on a day-to-day basis is an outstanding issue. South Africa, the first country in Africa to put biosafety laws in place (in 1997), has yet to develop a labelling process.

More public education and debate around GM food needs to happen, said Pinstrup-Andersen. "Almost all GM food varieties have been through stringent testing for health safety, which non-GM food has not undergone ever. People need to engage with the science and not the politics."

In Switzerland, Neither Farmers nor Consumers Want Genetically Modified Food

Bernard Nicod, as told to Luigi Jorio

In the following viewpoint, Luigi Jorio interviews Bernard Nicod, executive committee member of the Swiss Farmers' Association. Nicod contends that the Swiss public and Swiss farmers are not ready for genetically modified crops and food. Nicod claims that more needs to be known about the benefits and risks of genetic modification, as there are reasons for Switzerland to protect its agriculture industry. Jorio writes for Swissinfo.ch, the international branch of the Swiss Broadcasting Corporation (SBC).

As you read, consider the following questions:

1. Nicod claims that the production of genetically modified plants needs to meet what three conditions?
2. What cautionary tale does Nicod draw from farmers' experience with genetically modified crops in the United States?
3. According to Nicod, what would happen to organic agriculture in Switzerland if genetically modified crops were introduced?

The farming community in Switzerland is not opposed in principle to genetically modified (GM) plants. But growing GM plants is unthinkable in the present situation

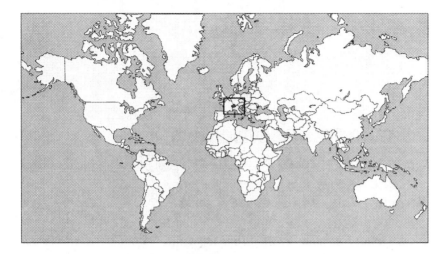

and the national moratorium should be extended till 2017, says the Swiss Farmers' Association.

GM plants are not harmful—neither for human health nor for the environment: that is the basic finding reached by the Swiss National Science Foundation's National Research Programme (NRP) on the risks and benefits of GM plants in agriculture.

In the present circumstances, however, the economic benefit of this biotechnology for farmers remains "modest", says the final report of NRP 59.

But apart from the economic evaluation of the researchers, what do farmers think of GM plants? And how do they evaluate the potential benefits and risks of growing them?

The Farmers' View

Swissinfo.ch spoke to Bernard Nicod, a member of the executive committee of the Swiss Farmers' Association who describes himself as a "typical lowland farmer" from canton Vaud.

Swissinfo.ch: You grow potatoes, cereals, forage and tobacco in the conventional manner. Would you be prepared to introduce GM plants on your farm?

Bernard Nicod: I am not opposed in principle to genetic engineering. Most of the farmers, at least those who belong to our association, share this view. We just think that Swiss agriculture is not ready for it yet.

The majority of our consumers do not want foods produced from transgenic crops.

For what reasons?

Production of genetically modified plants needs to meet three conditions: It has to make sense from an ecological, an agricultural and an economic point of view. Currently, none of these criteria hold.

Can you explain?

Swiss agriculture needs among other things to supply food products to consumers. Currently, the majority of our consumers do not want foods produced from transgenic crops. No businessperson would want to get into producing goods that the consumer doesn't want.

Switzerland is a small country, with farms and fields close together. So it would be hard to separate the cycle of production and distribution of conventional agriculture from that of transgenic agriculture. We are not sure we can cope with the extra costs of that kind of separation.

These costs, as well as the issue of legal liability in case of contamination, were not considered in the studies of NRP 59. This is another reason why research on GM plants should be continued so as to better define the problems from different points of view. We believe therefore that the moratorium on growing GM plants should be extended to 2017.

The Benefits and Risks

Just theoretically, what could be the advantages of growing GM plants in Switzerland?

Increase in productivity—in quantitative and even qualitative terms. I am thinking for example of the amount of protein or increased nutritional value of some transgenic plants. GM plants can resist diseases and parasites and thus reduce the need for pesticides and fungicides.

Climate change means that some crops may have to adapt to a new context. GM plants could contribute positively to adaptation to the climate—for example by better resisting water stress.

What do you fear as potential risks?

Most of all the lack of in-depth knowledge about the impact of GM plants on the environment. From the NRP 59 report it would appear that there are no problems, but I do not think the range of things considered was sufficient to reach that conclusion. It will be important to carry on the research to get more convincing answers.

The tools and materials of biotechnology are concentrated in the hands of one or two big multinationals whose ethical values may be different from those of our society. With GM plants, there is the risk of being beholden to whoever supplies seeds and products. The farmer would lose his independence.

We are seeing that in the US, where there are traditional farmers surrounded by transgenic operations. They have no choice but to join the trend.

In the particular case of Switzerland, it needs to be said that our farm products are exposed to strong competition from neighbouring countries. Today our products are still strong because we adhere to particular principles of cultivation, close to the land. The day we start growing GM plants, we are likely to disappear into the crowd and we will suffer economic losses.

Finally, it should be borne in mind that one of the tasks of farmers is to maintain biodiversity. But we know that using GM plants has the tendency to reduce the number of species. I can't help wondering if this is not a contradiction.

The Threat to Organic Farming

Organic farming in Switzerland is well developed: On average it involves one farm in ten. Can this coexist with GM crops?

With considerable difficulty. The rules for organic agriculture in Switzerland are very strict, especially when you compare them to those of neighbouring countries. If GM plants were introduced, it would become even more difficult to meet the organic criteria and the whole sector would be doomed to disappear.

Today our products are still strong because we adhere to particular principles of cultivation, close to the land.

Given how close fields are together, the risk of spreading and contamination is great. For example, we have farm machinery being used on different farms. To avoid any contamination, farmers would have to buy new machinery, or it would have to be thoroughly cleaned before every new job. But that is not economically feasible. Again, how could you be sure that the "GM" farmer who goes over to talk to his "organic" neighbour won't bring traces of pollen or seed on his boots?

So GM plants have no future in Switzerland?

It depends. Today our priority is to feed the world's population. If in the future other interests or issues emerge, to do with water supply for example, and if biotechnology provides a valid solution, I believe that Swiss farmers will be able to keep an open mind.

In the European Union, Opposition to Genetically Modified Food Is Not Reflected in Sales Data

European Commission

In the following viewpoint, the European Commission argues that the results of a study on European purchasing choices shows that although most people know that genetically modified food has to be labeled, the majority of consumers do not read the food label and do not try to avoid genetically modified food. The author contends that this shows that there is a market for genetically modified food in Europe, despite the widespread negative attitudes that people express. The European Commission is the European Union's executive body and represents the interests of Europe as a whole.

As you read, consider the following questions:

1. According to the author, what percentage of Europeans do not make any effort to identify genetically modified food products in order to avoid them?

2. What fraction of survey respondents did not know whether or not they buy genetically modified food, according to the European Commission?

Adapted from "Do European Consumers Buy GMO Foods?," *A Decade of EU-Funded GMO Research (2001–2010)*, 2010. © European Union, 1995–2013. Reproduced by permission.

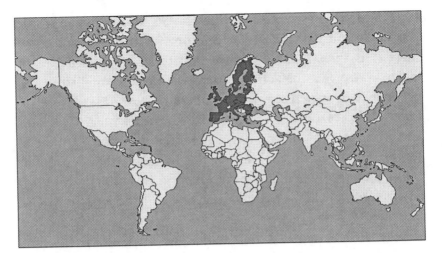

3. The author claims that a focus group study determined that which two issues are more important to consumers than genetically modified ingredients?

Following the 2004 adoption by the EU [European Union] of compulsory labelling of all food products containing GM [genetic modification] in any ingredient, it was uncertain how rapidly such products would appear on the shelves of retail grocery stores. It appeared that, at the end of 2005, labelled GM foods of one sort or another were on sale in various countries in Europe.

A Study of Purchasing Choices

During the past decade there have been numerous debates and campaigns focusing on genetically modified crops and their food products. Several public opinion polls and focus groups exploring public attitudes to GM-containing food products showed that a majority of the European public was somewhat antipathetic to the technology, with views ranging from some who were vigorously opposed, a proportion enthusiastically in favour, while most people were essentially disinterested.

These surveys were hypothetical in asking 'what would you do if you had the opportunity of buying GM products?' since it is questionable whether attitudes expressed can be taken as a proxy for action. There were a few small-scale experiments in which limited numbers of consumers were offered a choice between identical products with a GM label and without, but with a price differential in favour of the GM option. However, no exploration was made of what consumers actually choose when shopping for food in familiar stores offering food labelled as containing or being derived from GM ingredients.

During the past decade there have been numerous debates and campaigns focusing on genetically modified crops and their food products.

The prime strategic objectives of these studies were therefore to:

- determine the discrepancy between measured attitudes of European consumers towards GM foods and their actual purchases when they were given the opportunity to choose between GM and non-GM;

- record GM products offered for sale, how customers are informed by labelling, price and supplementary information, and product position and prominence on the shelves;

- supplement the findings with specific opinion polls and focus groups;

- provide reliable evidence of genuine consumer GM food choices to food chain stakeholders in order to help them in their future planning.

The ConsumerChoice project 'Do European consumers buy GM foods?' conducted a series of studies which included the exploration of purchasing choices in the Czech Republic, Estonia, Germany, Greece, The Netherlands, Poland, Slovenia, Spain, Sweden and the United Kingdom [UK]. . . .

GM-Labelled Products

During the period of the project the public debate on GM issues in Europe was generally relatively subdued, although markedly more active in some countries at particular times, such as in the UK in the summer of 2008 and in France earlier in the year. The tone of the media coverage changed during the period from negative-neutral to neutral–slightly positive.

The preparedness of supermarket managers to discuss the GM issue varied between individual companies as well as between countries. Most large supermarket chains were not willing to provide sales data on GM-labelled products. Small shopkeepers usually were unaware of the transgenic provenance of some of the products in their stores. However, none of them, large or small, reported any consumer reactions whatsoever.

We determined that GM-labelled products were on sale in Estonia, Poland, the Czech Republic, Spain, the Netherlands and the United Kingdom. In Slovenia, Greece, Germany and Sweden no GM-labelled products were found on the market during the period of the project. In those countries where GM-labelled foods were on sale, most were oils from GM soya or GM maize sold either as cooking oil or incorporated into other products such as margarine and crisps. We established that the number of GM-containing products on offer was considerably lower than before the introduction of the labelling regulation.

The Survey Results

The results of the two questionnaires to Europeans living in the US showed that most of them (92%) said they knew what

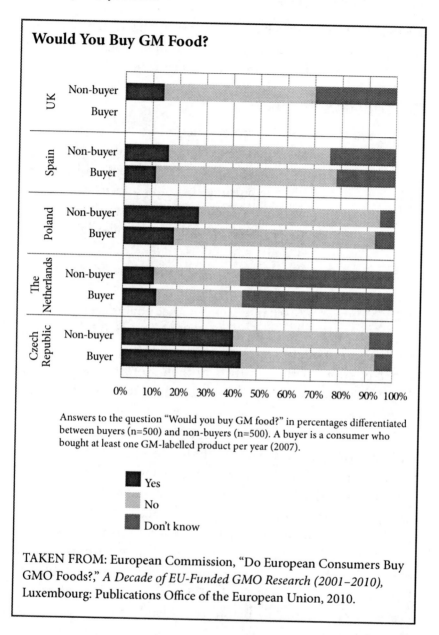

Would You Buy GM Food?

Answers to the question "Would you buy GM food?" in percentages differentiated between buyers (n=500) and non-buyers (n=500). A buyer is a consumer who bought at least one GM-labelled product per year (2007).

■ Yes
▨ No
■ Don't know

TAKEN FROM: European Commission, "Do European Consumers Buy GMO Foods?," *A Decade of EU-Funded GMO Research (2001–2010)*, Luxembourg: Publications Office of the European Union, 2010.

GM food was and more than half were aware that unlabelled GM foods are for sale in the US. However this knowledge failed to prompt most of them (73%) to make any effort to identify these products in order to avoid them.

For all the countries with GM-labelled products on sale, 75% of respondents claimed to know that these have to be labelled by law. Nearly 60% said they did not know how to distinguish a GM-containing product from a conventional one. Although not everyone read the detailed ingredients list before they bought a particular food item, 54.1% of respondents said they did. There was no significant difference between buyers and non-buyers in the answers to these three questions. More than half the respondents said they were not careful in avoiding GM-labelled food.

We determined that GM-labelled products were on sale in Estonia, Poland, the Czech Republic, Spain, the Netherlands and the United Kingdom.

Comparison of respondents' actual behaviour with their perceptions revealed no significant difference between buyers and non-buyers. Half the respondents (49.8%) said they *did not* buy GM-labelled food. Interestingly, 48% of GM buyers thought they *did not* buy GM-labelled food. Conversely, almost 23% of non-buyers thought they *did* buy GM-labelled food. A remarkably high number of respondents (30%) claimed not to know.

Focus group studies showed that GM food is not high in people's minds when discussing food purchasing habits. Labelling was demanded by participants, yet few of them actually looked at the labels when buying food. Sceptical arguments were more dominant than consideration of benefits but it seems likely that, in the future, climatic and population restraints on food availability may lead to greater acceptance of GM foods.

The Conclusions to Be Drawn

Overall these studies lead us to conclude that only a small number of GM-labelled products are for sale and purchased in various European countries. As the number of GM products available since the introduction of labelling has declined significantly, we can conclude that European consumers are restricted in their choice of purchases, reflecting the lack of availability of these products in the stores.

That three in four people claim to know that GM food has to be labelled, and that two-thirds say that they cannot distinguish GM from non-GM products, may reflect the fact that fewer than 50% of respondents bothered to read labels before buying a food item. Alternatively, it may mean that the information on the label is misunderstood or misinterpreted. Another reason may be that people are simply not interested: This seems to be confirmed by the finding that only 30% of respondents are careful never to buy foods with GM ingredients.

Our findings, including the studies of Polish and British residents living in the United States, suggest that most people are neither really interested in, nor very alert to, the presence of GM ingredients or products. Opinion polls elsewhere have shown a low and declining level of interest in the GM issue when respondents are asked unprompted to list their concerns about food. It is only when GMOs [genetically modified organisms] are brought specifically to their attention that they show antipathy. This is also confirmed by the results of the focus group discussions.

A Difference Between Actions and Words

By and large, consumers continue to display a negative attitude towards genetically modified ingredients in food products and gene technology in particular. When asked whether they would buy GM foods, supposing such benefits as lower prices, healthier or tastier products, or production under 'environmentally-friendly' regimes, most people remained negative. This is not reflected in the focus group results, where people seemed more positive about GM foods with specific benefits. The focus group study leads us to conclude that genetically modified ingredients are not an issue that people consider seriously while shopping. Care for the environment or quality in proportion to price are more important. It would be interesting to explore the reasons for such differences further.

The fact that GM-labelled products are available and actually bought shows that there is indeed a market for such products. Our results may suggest that this market might be even larger than believed, as 20% of non-buyers thought they were already buying GM foods, and around 30% did not even know whether or not they were doing so. Interestingly, the data showed no significant differences between buyers and non-buyers.

Our findings . . . suggest that most people are neither really interested in, nor very alert to, the presence of GM ingredients or products.

Our observations underline the fact that what people say differs from what they do. When asked whether they had bought GM food, half of our respondents said they had not. Yet the bar code analyses of their purchases showed that half of them were wrong and that they had indeed bought such products. Perhaps they did not know what they had bought. Some people also thought they had bought GM food when, in fact, they had not. Our data is not sufficiently extensive to probe more deeply into the minds of the shoppers but we may reasonably conclude that:

- most people do not actively avoid GM food, suggesting that they are not greatly concerned with the GM issue;

- linking purchasing data with answers to questionnaires is a more reliable way to establish attitudes than just opinion polls.

In India, Government May Criminalize Protest Against Genetically Modified Food

Ranjit Devraj

In the following viewpoint, Ranjit Devraj contends that there is much controversy over the introduction of genetically modified food in India and, in particular, about a proposed law that may stifle dissent. Devraj explains that although the project to introduce genetically modified bananas faces stiff opposition, there are also those who argue that the bananas could help solve one of India's big health problems. Devraj is regional editor for the Inter Press Service (IPS).

As you read, consider the following questions:

1. What percentage of Indian people are involved in agricultural activities, according to Devraj?
2. According to the author, India produces and consumes what amount of bananas annually?
3. The author cites studies finding what fraction of Indian women have anemia, or iron deficiency?

India's environmental and food security activists who have so far succeeded in stalling attempts to introduce genetically modified (GM) food crops into this largely farming country now find themselves up against a bill in parliament that could criminalise such opposition.

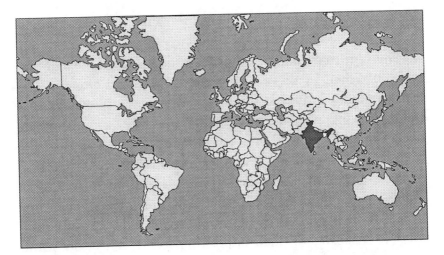

A Proposed Law

The Biotechnology Regulatory Authority of India (BRAI) bill, introduced into parliament in April [2013], provides for 'single window clearance' for projects by biotechnology and agribusiness companies including those to bring GM food crops into this country, 70 percent of whose 1.1 billion people are involved in agricultural activities.

"Popular opposition to the introduction of GM crops is the result of a campaign launched by civil society groups to create awareness among consumers," said Devinder Sharma, food security expert and leader of the Forum for Biotechnology and Food Security. "Right now we are opposing a plan to introduce GM bananas from Australia."

Sharma told IPS [Inter Press Service] that if the BRAI bill becomes law such awareness campaigns will attract stiff penalties. The bill provides for jail terms and fines for "whoever, without any evidence or scientific record misleads the public about the safety of organisms and products. . . ."

Suman Sahai, who leads 'Gene Campaign', an organisation dedicated to the conservation of genetic resources and indigenous knowledge, told IPS that "this draconian bill has been introduced in parliament without taking into account evidence constantly streaming in from around the world about the safety risks posed by GM food crops."

She said that Indian activists are now studying a new report published in the peer-reviewed *Journal of Organic Systems* by Judy Carman at Flinders University in Adelaide, Australia, showing evidence that pigs fed on GM corn and soy are likely to develop severe stomach inflammation.

"The new bill is not about regulation, but the promotion of the interests of food giants trying to introduce risky technologies into India, ignoring the rights of farmers and consumers," Sahai said. "It is alarming because it gives administrators the power to quell opposition to GM technology and criminalise those who speak up against it."

India's environmental and food security activists . . . now find themselves up against a bill in parliament that could criminalise such opposition.

The Introduction of GM Bananas

The past month has seen stiff opposition to plans to introduce GM bananas into India by a group of leading NGOs [nongovernmental organisations] that includes the Initiative for Health & Equity in Society, Guild for Services, Azadi Bachao Andolan, Save Honey Bees Campaign, Navdanya and Gene Ethics in Australia.

These groups are seeking cancellation of a deal between the Queensland University of Technology (QUT) and India's biotechnology department to grow GM bananas here.

Vandana Shiva, who leads the biodiversity conservation organisation Navdanya, and is among India's top campaigners against GM crops, told IPS that such food crop experiments pose a "direct threat to India's biodiversity, seed sovereignty, indigenous knowledge and public health by gradually replacing diverse crop varieties with a few patented monocultures."

She fears that an attempt is being made to control the cultivation of bananas in India through patents by "powerful men in distant places, who are totally ignorant of the biodiversity in our fields."

India produces and consumes 30 million tonnes of bananas annually, followed by Uganda which produces 12 million tonnes and consumes the fruit as a staple.

India's National Research Centre for Banana (NRCB), which has preserved more than 200 varieties of the fruit, is a partner in the GM banana project. Others include the Indian Institute of Horticultural Research, the Bhabha Atomic Research Centre (BARC) and Tamil Nadu Agricultural University.

With so much official involvement there are fears that GM bananas may eventually find their way into nutrition programmes run by the government. "There is a danger that GM bananas will be introduced into such programmes as the integrated child development scheme and the midday meals for children," Shiva said.

India's Integrated Child Development Services (ICDS), the world's largest integrated early childhood programme, began in 1975 and now covers 4.8 million expectant and nursing mothers and over 23 million children under the age of six. Bananas are included as part of the meals served in many of the 40,000 feeding centres.

A Proponent of the Project

QUT's Prof. James Dale, who leads the project, has, in interviews given to Australian media, justified the GM experiment by saying that it will "save Indian women from childbirth death due to iron deficiency."

According to studies conducted by the International Institute for Population Sciences in Mumbai, more than 50 percent of Indian women and more than 55 percent of pregnant women in India are anaemic. It is estimated that 25 percent of maternal deaths are due to complications arising out of anaemia.

In a Mar. 9, 2012, interview with the Australian Broadcasting Corporation, Dale said, "One of the major reasons around iron is that a large proportion of the Indian population are vegetarians and it's very difficult in a vegetarian diet to have intake of sufficient iron, particularly for subsistence farming populations.

"India is the largest producer of bananas in the world but they don't export any; all of them are consumed locally. So it's a very good target to be able to increase the amount of iron in bananas that can then be distributed to . . . the poor and subsistence farmers."

Dale denied in the interview that there were risks to existing Indian banana strains and said because bananas were sterile there is no danger that the genes being introduced will enter and destroy other varieties.

The Ongoing Controversy

But experts like Shiva have challenged Dale's claim. She said Australian scientists are using a virus that infects the banana as a promoter and that this could spread through horizontal gene transfer.

"All genetic modification uses genes from bacteria and viruses and various studies have shown that there are serious health risks associated with GM foods," she stressed, adding that there are safer, cheaper and more natural ways to add iron to diets.

India is the world's biggest grower of fruits and vegetables with many varieties naturally rich in iron. "Good sources of dietary iron in India include turmeric, lotus stem, coconut, mango (and) amaranth. . . . There is no need to genetically modify banana, a sacred plant in India," she said.

Attempts by IPS to contact Dale directly and separately through QUT's press relations department on the risks from horizontal gene transfer and the possible danger to public health failed to elicit any response.

According to Shiva there is a concerted move by food corporations to control important food crops and staples in their centres of origin. "We have seen GM corn introduced into Mexico and there was a determined attempt to introduce GM brinjal in India."

India is the world's biggest grower of fruits and vegetables.

In February 2010, the then minister for environment, Jairam Ramesh, ordered a moratorium on the brinjal project and his action was seen as a major blow to the introduction of GM food crops in India.

"If the new bill is passed, we could have a reversed situation and projects like GM bananas will be quickly cleared with the backing of the government—and it will only be a matter of time before India becomes a GM banana republic," Sharma said.

In Asia, There Is Ambivalence Toward Genetically Modified Crops

Wang Zichen and Liu Tong

In the following viewpoint, Wang Zichen and Liu Tong argue that public opinion and policy on the issue of genetically modified food vary across China, Japan, and Korea, as well as the Association of Southeast Asian Nations of Indonesia, Malaysia, the Philippines, Singapore, Thailand, Brunei, Burma (Myanmar), Cambodia, Laos, and Vietnam. The authors state that many countries have restrictions on the technology due to safety concerns. Zichen and Tong write for Xinhuanet, a Chinese news agency that publishes in eight languages.

As you read, consider the following questions:

1. According to the authors, how many people in Asia are suffering from hunger?
2. In what two countries is the farming of genetically modified crops forbidden, according to Zichen and Tong?
3. How many million tons of genetically modified soybeans does China import annually, according to the authors?

The role of genetic modification (GM) technology in Asian agriculture remains unclear and individual countries have adopted different approaches to tackle the sensitive subject.

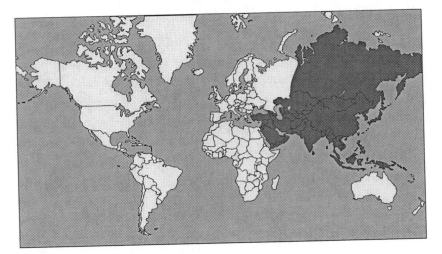

A Lack of Consensus

At a food security meeting held by ASEAN [Association of Southeast Asian Nations] Plus Three (APT) countries this week [July 10, 2013], participants from ASEAN countries, China, Japan and the Republic of Korea (ROK) showed ambivalence toward GM technology.

The 13 countries, with a combined population of over 2 billion people, rely heavily on agricultural production and have a significant part of their population devoted to growing crops.

Meanwhile, 560 million people in Asia are suffering from hunger.

Leonardo Montemayor, president of the Federation of Free Farmers of the Philippines, said an increasing number of people in his country have started planting GM corn after realizing that the corn is more resistant to pests and diseases.

However, Dao The Anh, director of Vietnam's Center for Agrarian Systems Research and Development, has voiced concern about the social and economic consequences GM crops could bring, including their potential impact on biodiversity.

As supplies of genetically engineered seeds are monopolized by a few corporations, some farmers worry about maintaining sustainable access to GM technology, as well as possible future price hikes that could render the seeds unaffordable for poor farmers.

Pornsil Patchrintanakul, vice chairman of the Thai Chamber of Commerce, said there is no consensus among the ASEAN community regarding GM crops, adding that the countries are divided on the adoption and popularization of GM technology.

Growing GM crops is forbidden in Thailand, Patchrintanakul added.

GM Food in China

This is also the case in China. The world's biggest grain producer maintains a standing policy that forbids growing GM grain.

But China does allow imports of certain GM products. In 2012, China imported over 58 million tons of soybeans—mostly genetically modified—a practice that has been going on for years.

Public opinions on GM crops in China are polarized, with a great number of people holding suspicions toward GM products.

Rao Yi, a renowned professor and dean of Peking University's School of Life Sciences, said that while some GM-related concerns still need to be discussed, there are also rumors that need to be dispelled.

"There have not been detrimental effects to human health from GM organisms. Because these organisms are so diverse, everything has to be judged on a case-by-case basis," said Brett Rierson, United Nations World Food Programme (WFP) representative to China.

According to a paper issued by the World Health Organization, "GM foods currently available on the international market have passed risk assessments and are not likely to present risks for human health. In addition, no effects on human health have been shown as a result of the consumption of such foods by the general population in the countries where they have been approved."

There are also economic issues at play. Domestically grown soybeans are scarce in China, as China's imports of GM soybeans rocketed to 58 million tons from less than 3 million tons in 1997. Many farmers have abandoned soybeans for other crops, as imported soybeans are cheaper in price.

Diverse cultures and religions span across these countries and reservations about GM are sometimes based on religious or cultural beliefs.

"GM is difficult to discuss in the Chinese media (and with the Chinese public). The discourse has been greatly distorted by extremists. The media has been influenced by them," Rao said.

GM technology is the future of agriculture, said Fang Zhouzi, a biochemist and vocal supporter of GM technology, adding that it will be harder for China to catch up with the U.S., which already has advanced GM technology, if China does not recognize this fact.

But safety concerns apparently have not been ruled out by APT countries, which include some of the world's biggest producers, importers and exporters of agricultural products. Diverse cultures and religions span across these countries and reservations about GM are sometimes based on religious or cultural beliefs.

Getachew Diriba, country director at WFP, said the organization has no opinion regarding GM. "But it's out there, it's being used. It is up to individual countries to exactly determine when to use and when not to use it," he said.

Periodical and Internet Sources Bibliography

The following articles have been selected to supplement the diverse views presented in this chapter.

Agence France Presse	"Mexico Approves GM Maize Pilot Project," March 9, 2011.
Leo Cendrowicz	"Is Europe Finally Ready for Genetically Modified Foods?," *Time*, March 9, 2010.
Kate Connolly	"Germany Deals Blow to GM Crops," *Guardian* (UK), April 14, 2009.
Natalie DeGraaf	"Changing Seeds, or Seeds of Change?," *GeneWatch*, October–November 2011.
Economist	"The Adoption of Genetically Modified Crops: Growth Areas," February 23, 2011.
Andrew Grice	"GM Crops: Public Fears over 'Frankenstein Food' May Be Easing, *Independent* Poll Reveals," *Independent* (UK), July 23, 2013.
Afua Hirsch	"GM Crops: Campaigners in Ghana Accuse US of Pushing Modified Food," *Guardian* (UK), July 24, 2013.
Eric Hoffman	"Food, Made from Scratch," *GeneWatch*, January–March 2013.
Independent (UK)	"Genetically-Modified Food for Thought," August 11, 2009.
Louise Lucas, Joshua Chaffin, and Jim Pickard	"UK Set for GM Food Push in Europe," *Financial Times* (UK), March 8, 2013.
Spiegel Online	"'Consumers Aren't Ready for GM Crops': Food Companies Say No to Genetically Modified Potatoes," April 27, 2010.

CHAPTER 2

The Impact of Genetically Modified Crops on Agriculture

Food Fight

Roger Beachy, as told to Brendan Borrell

In the following viewpoint, Roger Beachy, interviewed by Brendan Borrell, claims that genetically modified crops have many benefits, including allowing farmers to use less pesticides and herbicides, thus lessening the environmental pollution from agriculture. Beachy claims that although there are some risks with genetically modified crops, these must be balanced by considering the many benefits. Beachy is former director of the National Institute of Food and Agriculture (NIFA) at the US Department of Agriculture (USDA). Borrell is a journalist.

As you read, consider the following questions:

1. According to Borrell, what percentages of soybean and corn crops in the United States are genetically engineered?
2. According to Beachy, agriculture and forestry account for what percentage of global greenhouse emissions?
3. What is the benefit of rice genetically modified to contain more vitamin A, according to Beachy?

Roger Beachy grew up in a traditional Amish family on a small farm in Ohio that produced food "in the old ways," he says, with few insecticides, herbicides or other agrochemicals. He went on to become a renowned expert in plant viruses and sowed the world's first genetically modified food crop—a tomato plant with a gene that conferred resistance to the devastating tomato mosaic virus. Beachy sees no irony between his rustic, low-tech boyhood and a career spent developing new types of agricultural technologies. For him, genetic manipulation of food plants is a way of helping preserve the traditions of small farms by reducing the amount of chemicals farmers have to apply to their crops.

In 2009 Beachy took the helm of the National Institute of Food and Agriculture, a new research arm of the U.S. Department of Agriculture, where he controls a $1.5 billion budget for pursuing his vision of the future of agriculture. In the past year Beachy's institute has funded ambitious agricultural research, such as a massive genomic study of 5,000 lines of wheat and barley, alongside unexpected projects: a $15 million behavioral study on childhood obesity in rural states, for one.

Beachy's appointment sparked controversy among environmentalists because his work helped to kick-start the $11 billion global agricultural biotechnology industry. Seed companies never commercialized his virus-resistant plants, but their success—tomato plants that showed near complete resistance to multiple virus strains—underlined the potential for a technology that was ultimately widely embraced by U.S. farmers. Today in the U.S. more than 90 percent of soybean and cotton crops and more than 80 percent of corn plants are genetically engineered to resist herbicides and insects using methods similar to the ones developed by Beachy. Organic farmers and locavores worry about Beachy's ties to big agriculture—much of his tomato work received funding from Monsanto—and his advocacy of genetic modification of food crops. Beachy, though, remains unrepentant. Although he believes seed companies can do more to improve food security in the developing world, he insists that genetic manipulation is essential to feed the earth's growing population sustainably. Edited excerpts of a phone conversation with Beachy follow.

SCIENTIFIC AMERICAN: *Did you actually get to see the first GM tomatoes when they were planted in the field in Illinois in 1987?*

BEACHY: Oh, my goodness, I planted them. I went out and hoed them. I was out there once a week looking at everything in the field, and my daughter K.C. even helped me weed the tomato patch one time. I really wanted to observe the patch and see how it was progressing.

Were you surprised by how effective the virus-resistance gene was?

Absolutely. As the parental plants without the resistance gene were getting sicker and sicker, the ones that had the gene looked just dynamite. I still have the original photos from 25 years ago, and it's pretty remarkable even now to look at them and say, "By George, our stuff really works!" Other people have seen the same kind of technology work in cucumbers and papaya and squash and green peppers; many are surprised at how relatively simple the concept was and yet how much of an impact it can have.

What we've gotten over the past 15 to 20 years is a considerable amount of insecticides not being used in the environment.

That effectiveness does not last forever, of course. Today we are seeing the resistance these technologies provide against pests and disease being overcome. Do you think the industry has relied too much on GM as a "silver bullet"?

No, these things happen in plant breeding of all kinds, whether it's traditional breeding or molecular breeding like we're doing now. In the 1960s and 1970s new types of wheat rust spread up from Mexico on the wind, and the plant breeders would hustle and hustle to find resistance to one strain of rust, and then, several years later, another strain would come, so they would have to be looking ahead to find any new resistance.

Durable, permanent resistance is almost unheard of, which brings up the question of why did we create GM crops in the first place? What we've gotten over the past 15 to 20 years is a considerable amount of insecticides not being used in the environment. That's remarkable. What we're wondering now is if we will go back to using only chemicals or if we will be able to find new genes that will capture the diversity of pests that we're seeing around the world.

Unlike in the U.S., tropical regions of the world, including parts of China, face constant pressure from multiple insects. To control the variety of crop-damaging insects, scientists will need a variety of different genetic technologies, or it may be necessary to apply nongenetic technologies, such as different proven insecticides to control them. Overall, we'll find the kinds of genes that will protect against white flies in one country and aphids in another country. If we manage this right, we'll have the genetic solutions to these questions and not chemical solutions and will therefore, in my opinion, be more sustainable.

Critics of the agricultural biotechnology industry complain that it has focused on providing benefits to farmers rather than improving foods for consumers. What do you say to them?

In the early years many of us in the university community were looking at using genetic engineering to enhance vitamin content of foods, improve the quality of seed proteins and develop crops that don't require use of pesticides—all things we thought would benefit agriculture and consumers. The process for approval of a biotechnology product was onerous, expensive and unknown for academics. It would take the private sector to make the new technologies successful and find an opportunity to give farmers crops with higher productivity. But the food companies that purchased these crops—General Mills, Kellogg's—were not used to paying more for wheat or oats that had more nutritional content or for vegetables that were higher in minerals.

The Benefits to Farmers

Many farmers who use GE [genetically engineered] crops have experienced more cost-effective weed control and reduced losses from insect pests. Farmers who previously faced high levels of insect pests that were difficult to treat before insect-resistant crops have particularly benefited from applying lower amounts of or less expensive insecticides. More effective management of weeds and insects also means that farmers may not have to apply insecticides or till for weeds as often, translating into lower expenditures for pesticides and less labor and fuel for equipment operations.

National Academies,
"The Impact of Genetically Engineered Crops on
Farm Sustainability in the United States,"
Report in Brief, *2010.*

Why not?

Because the American public would not be willing to pay more for those products.

Today consumers are willing to pay more for crops that are labeled "organic" or even "GM-free" because they view them as more sustainable. How do you think GM crops can help make agriculture more sustainable?

In my opinion, the GM crops we have today already contributed to sustainable agriculture. They have reduced the use of harmful pesticides and herbicides and the loss of soils because they promote the use of no-till methods of farming. Nevertheless, there is much more that can be done. As you know, agriculture and forestry account for approximately 31 percent of global greenhouse gas emissions, larger than the 26 percent from the energy sector. Agriculture is a major source of emissions of methane and nitrous oxides and is responsible for some of the pollution of waterways because of fertilizer runoff from fields. Agriculture needs to do better.

We haven't reached the plateau of global population and may not until 2050 or 2060. In the interim, we must increase food production while reducing greenhouse gas emissions and soil erosion and decrease pollution of waterways. That's a formidable challenge. With new technologies in seeds and in crop production, it will be possible to reduce the use of chemical fertilizers and the amount of irrigation while maintaining high yields. Better seeds will help, as will improvements in agricultural practices.

Environmentalists have been reluctant to embrace GM crops because of concerns about genes flowing to non-GM crops and also to wild native plants. That's one reason a federal judge in California recently ordered genetically modified sugar beets to be destroyed.

You are correct. Nevertheless, it is important to note that the court ruling is not about the safety of the sugar beets or the plants that result from cross-pollination. The farmers who brought suit charge a premium for their crops because they are branded as organic—a definition that does not include genetic engineering. They are worried that their non-GM crops will be pollinated by pollen from GM crops, reducing their value. In this case, it is not an issue of food safety but of product marketing.

The GM crops we have today already contributed to sustainable agriculture.

On the other hand, it's true that there are reasons why we want to preserve wild populations of crop plants: They act as a reservoir for genetic diversity. Here in the U.S., we are not, for instance, planting GM corn alongside wild maize, which is from Mexico. There are some native species for which there is a cross-pollination possibility, for example, squashes and melons, where there are some wild progenitors out in the field. It will be important to ensure that such germplasm is preserved.

In some quarters it might actually be seen as positive if a trait for disease or pest resistance, whether or not it was of GM origin, was transferred to weedy relatives, because it will reduce pests or pathogens in the area.

It may be a positive thing for agriculture, but not necessarily for wild ecosystems. What are the consequences if you create a vitamin A–rich rice and that gene spreads into an environment where vitamin A is scarce?

Most scientists do not predict any negative consequences if the genes used to develop Golden Rice [vitamin A–rich rice] are transferred to other varieties or to wild relatives. In contrast, the payoff for making Golden Rice widely available to those with vitamin A–poor diets is enormous. Imagine if we further delayed the release of such improved foods, leaving many hundreds of thousands of children with blindness and impaired vision and early deaths because of deficiency of vitamin A. What is the value of sight in children? What is the potential damage should the genetic trait be transferred to wild or feral rice? You're right—you can't say that every place in the country or every place in the world or every environment, hot or cold, that it won't have an impact, but we need to weigh the risks and benefits.

Some scientists have complained that biotech companies have stymied research on GM crops. Aren't these studies needed to get accurate answers about the risks of these crops?

That's a complex question with many different factors at play. In my opinion, the field would be more advanced if more academic scientists were involved in testing and other types of experimentation. We've had too little involvement of the academic sector in some of these cases. Many of us urged early on that there be more sharing, and I can understand the concerns of the academics.

On the other hand, I've asked companies why seed isn't made readily available for academic scientists' use. Some point out that there have been a number of academic studies in the past 20 years about using GM crops that were incomplete or poorly designed. And as a result, there was a lot of wasted effort by many other scientists that follow up on such studies.

I hope that the future brings greater collaboration and less suspicion between public-sector and private-sector scientists in agriculture biotechnology.

Take the case of the report that pollen from insect-resistant corn harms larvae of Monarch and other butterflies, which led many to conclude that GM corn would have a devastating effect on Monarch populations. This finding was widely quoted in the media, and the USDA spent a great deal of energy and investment on follow-up research, which in the end showed that Monarch larvae were likely to be affected under very restricted conditions: for example, if the pollination of a crop occurs at the same time and place as the larval growth of the butterfly—a very, very rare occasion.

Furthermore, because the use of insect-resistant corn reduced the use of chemical pesticides, the outcome increased the population of butterflies and other insects. From this and other examples, companies were justifiably concerned about the quality of some academic studies and felt that they had more to lose than to gain in such cases. Yet there is much to be gained from academic scientists conducting well-designed studies with GM crops, and I hope that the future brings greater collaboration and less suspicion between public-sector and private-sector scientists in agriculture biotechnology.

What would be the consequence if GM crops were suddenly removed from the market?

Here in the U.S., there would likely be a modest increase in food prices because the efficiency of food production is currently high as a consequence of using GM traits, resulting in low food prices. We would have to go back to older types of production that would result in lower density of planting and likely lower per-acre outputs. We would likely see an increase in acreage planted, including the use of some marginal lands to increase total output. In the U.S. and other countries, there would be a significant increase in the use of agrochemicals, and the related health issues associated with such use would increase. Although there have been great advances in plant breeding during the past 20 years, the yields of the major commodity crops, such as maize, soybeans and cotton, would be less in the absence of biotechnology than with it. If total global crop production drops, the impacts would, of course, be greater on poorer nations than on those that are wealthier. The agriculturally poor countries would certainly suffer more than those that have a strong foundation of food agriculture production.

In the United States, Genetically Modified Crops Harm Farmers by Contaminating Crops

Food & Water Watch

In the following viewpoint, Food & Water Watch argues that non–genetically modified and organic food crops are increasingly being contaminated by genetically engineered crops, resulting in serious economic losses. The organization claims that farmers should have the ability to hold biotechnology companies liable for damages when contamination occurs. Food & Water Watch is a nonprofit organization that advocates for policies that will result in healthy and safe food, as well as access to safe and affordable drinking water.

As you read, consider the following questions:

1. According to Food & Water Watch, what is the estimated annual loss to organic farmers from market rejection?

2. Which two countries have banned certain US imports because of contamination, according to the author?

3. By 2007, how many lawsuits had Monsanto filed against US farmers for patent infringement, according to the author?

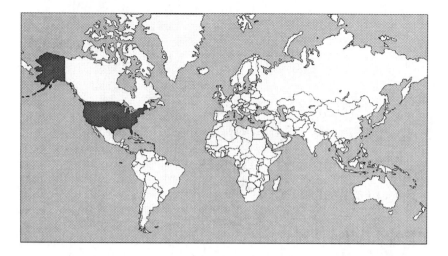

Genetically engineered (GE) crops now dominate commodity crop production in the United States. GE varieties make up 88 percent of corn acres, 94 percent of soybean acres and 90 percent of cotton acres planted in the country. With the rise of GE crops, coexistence between organic, non-GE and GE production has become more difficult due to the potential for gene flow and commingling of crops at both the planting and harvesting levels.

In official government jargon, this mixing is referred to as "adventitious presence," but what it means is that GE crops can contaminate non-GE and organic crops through cross-pollination on the field or through seed or grain mixing after harvest. Not only does GE contamination affect seed purity, but it also has serious ramifications for organic and non-GE farmers that face economic harm due to lost markets or decreased crop values.

Farmers Face Economic Loss

The financial burden associated with GE contamination is significant. Some of the costs to non-GE and organic farmers include the loss of market access, risks to long-term investments associated with the crop or one type of production, and the expense of putting in place preventative measures to avoid contamination. Preventative measures include creating buffer zones around fields, which can result in reduced crop yield; record-keeping; testing and surveillance of a crop; and segregation, maintenance and cleaning during all steps of the supply chain.

Additionally, consumers who are interested in buying non-GE foods know that they can rely on organic and non-GE labeled food products, but the threat of contamination reduces the confidence that consumers have in those products. The undermining of consumer confidence is yet another cost of contamination—or even of just the threat of contamination.

Farmers who intentionally grow GE crops are not required to plant non-GE buffer zones to prevent contamination unless this is stipulated in the farm's permit from the U.S. Department of Agriculture (USDA). Yet even the use of buffer zones has proven ineffective because these areas are usually not large enough to prevent contamination.

The financial burden associated with GE contamination is significant.

Data gathered by the Organic Trade Association illustrates that some grain buyers reject loads of crops that have a more than 0.9 percent GE presence, resulting in 0.25 percent of non-GE soybean loads and 3.5 percent of non-GE corn loads being rejected. A rejection by the load's intended buyer means a lost premium for that non-GE product. The estimated loss from market rejections alone is $40 million annually.

A Threat to the Business

Organic dairy farmers already face difficulty securing organic feed, and this challenge will only worsen if GE alfalfa begins to contaminate organic alfalfa. The USDA's approval of

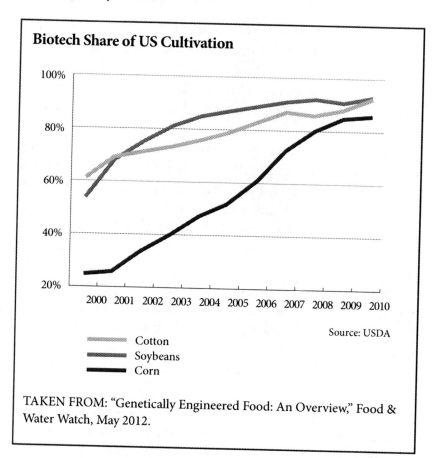

Biotech Share of US Cultivation

Source: USDA

Cotton
Soybeans
Corn

TAKEN FROM: "Genetically Engineered Food: An Overview," Food & Water Watch, May 2012.

Roundup Ready alfalfa in 2010 highlights the significant ramifications that contamination can have for organic producers. Alfalfa is the most important feed crop for dairy cows. Organic dairy farmers receive a price premium for their milk, but they also have production costs of $5 to $7 more per hundred pounds of milk—38 percent higher than for conventional dairies. If GE contamination eliminates this premium, which is mostly eaten up by higher organic production costs, these farms could be unprofitable.

Growers of non-GE and organic sugar beets and related crops—like table beets and chard—also face the possibility of contamination from nearby Roundup Ready sugar beet growers, as well as the potential economic effects associated with a tainted harvest. Over 50 percent of U.S. sugar beet seed production occurs in Oregon's Willamette Valley, also home to about half of the country's Swiss chard seed production. The Willamette Valley Specialty Seed Association requires that GE plants remain three miles from non-GE chard and beet seed producers, yet sugar beet pollen has been known to travel as far as five miles.

If contaminated, farmers producing non-GE and organic crops can also lose access to international markets. Many other countries have stricter GE regulations and labeling requirements than the United States. Despite the advanced U.S. grain-handling system, GE grains have contaminated non-GE shipments and devastated U.S. exports.

GE contamination of non-GE and organic fields is a growing problem in the United States that will only intensify with the approval of more GE crops.

The Government Accountability Office identified six known unauthorized releases of GE crops between 2000 and 2008. In 2000, Japan discovered GE StarLink corn, which was not approved for human food, in 70 percent of tested samples, even though StarLink represented under one percent of U.S. corn cultivation. After the StarLink discovery, the European Union [EU] banned all U.S. corn imports, costing U.S. farmers $300 million. In August 2006, unapproved GE LibertyLink rice was found to have contaminated conventional rice stocks. Japan halted all U.S. rice imports and the EU imposed heavy restrictions, costing the U.S. rice industry $1.2 billion.

The Legal Implications of Contamination

Besides the threat of economic harm from contamination, farmers who unintentionally grow patented GE seeds or who harvest crops that are cross-pollinated with GE traits could face costly lawsuits by biotechnology firms for "seed piracy."

By 2007, Monsanto had filed 112 lawsuits against U.S. farmers for patent infringement, recovering between $85.7 and $160.6 million. At least one farmer contends that he was sued when his canola fields were contaminated with GE crops from neighboring farms.

GE contamination of non-GE and organic fields is a growing problem in the United States that will only intensify with the approval of more GE crops. To help preserve diverse agricultural production methods, biotechnology companies that patent GE seeds should take responsibility for any financial harm that the presence of their patented technology inflicts upon non-GE and organic farmers.

Right now, if farmers are harmed by contamination or loss of their markets, it is virtually impossible for them to recover from these damages. The federal government has not dealt with this burden, even as the USDA continues to approve a steady stream of new GE crops. Congress and state legislatures must address the issue of liability for contamination by GE crops and require that the costs of GE contamination be borne by the biotech companies that created the technology and hold the patents on these seeds.

In Africa, Genetic Modification Can Solve Many Agricultural Challenges

Calestous Juma

In the following viewpoint, Calestous Juma claims that new challenges demand that biotechnologies be employed to solve problems. Juma contends that Africa is not reaping the full benefits of transgenic, or genetically modified, agriculture. He proposes that steps be taken to foster agricultural innovation to help promote adoption of this biotechnology. Juma is director of the Science, Technology, and Globalization Project at the Belfer Center for Science and International Affairs at Harvard University's John F. Kennedy School of Government.

As you read, consider the following questions:

1. According to Juma, in what year did emerging economies overtake industrialized nations as the main adopters of genetically modified crops?

2. Of the twenty-eight countries with transgenic crops, which four are in Africa, according to the author?

3. According to Juma, what are two possible ways to help foster agricultural innovation in Africa?

Calestous Juma, "How Africa Can Feed the World," *Globe and Mail*, June 3, 2013. Copyright © by Calestous Juma 2013. All rights reserved. Reproduced by permission. The author wishes to acknowledge the Gates Foundation and the International Development Research Centre of Canada for supporting the production of this article.

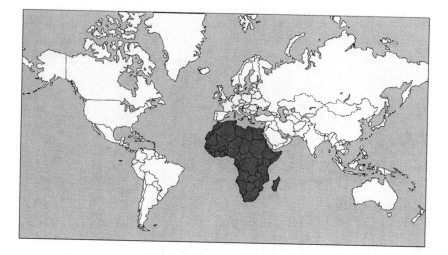

Neglect of agriculture has been a defining feature of Africa's economic policy over the last four decades. The future is more promising. Today Africa has become a major destination of agricultural foreign direct investment.

For example, Grow Africa, a consortium of foreign firms, has pledged to invest $3.5 billion in eight African countries. Grow Africa, seeded at the World Economic Forum, operates under the political guidance of the African Union with the technical support of the New Partnership for Africa's Development (NEPAD) agency.

Fostering sustainable agriculture in Africa will require significant investment in infrastructure, technical training (especially for women), creation of regional markets and the use of new technologies.

The Growth in Genetically Modified (GM) Crops

New challenges such as climate change and diversification of food sources demand the use of available technologies. New farm methods such as genetic modification, however, continue to generate considerable debate.

When GM crops were first commercially released in 1996, critics argued that they would only benefit industrialized countries. In 2012 emerging economies overtook industrialized countries as the main adopters of GM crops.

According to the International Service for the Acquisition of Agri-Biotech Applications [ISAAA], from 1996 to 2011 transgenic crops added $98.2 billion to the value of global agricultural output, over 50 per cent of which accrued to emerging economies.

The use of transgenic crops has reduced the use of active pesticide ingredients by nearly 473 million kg [kilograms]. It also reduced carbon dioxide emissions by 23.1 billion kilograms, the equivalent of taking 10.2 million cars off the road.

New challenges such as climate change and diversification of food sources demand the use of available technologies.

Without transgenic crops, the world would have needed another 108.7 million hectares of land for the same level of output. The benefits to biological diversity from this technology have therefore been invaluable. On the economic front, nearly 15 million farmers and their families, estimated at 50 million people, have benefited from the adoption of transgenic crops.

But not all the regions of the world are reaping the full benefits of agricultural biotechnology. Of the 28 countries growing transgenic crops, only four (South Africa, Burkina Faso, Egypt, and Sudan) are in Africa.

The Promise of New Biotechnology

Despite the initial slow pace of biotechnology adoption, the leapfrogging that occurred in mobile phones is on the verge of repeating itself in agricultural biotechnology. This is a result

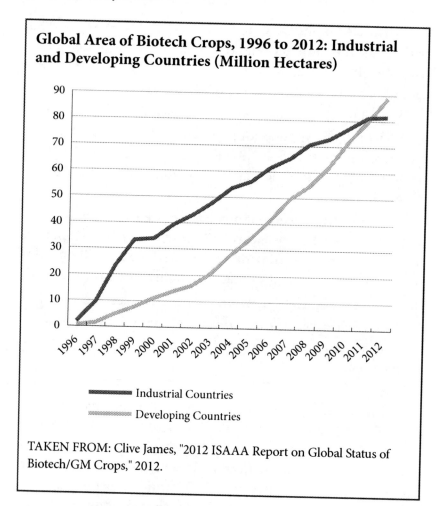

Global Area of Biotech Crops, 1996 to 2012: Industrial and Developing Countries (Million Hectares)

Industrial Countries
Developing Countries

TAKEN FROM: Clive James, "2012 ISAAA Report on Global Status of Biotech/GM Crops," 2012.

of the increasing capacity among African countries to absorb existing biotechnologies and use them to solve local problems.

Two examples underscore this point. In Nigeria scientists have developed a pest-resistant variety of the black-eyed pea, a subspecies of the cowpea (*Vigna unguiculata*), to control the insect *Maruca vitrata*. The pest destroys nearly $300 million worth of the crop annually. Pesticides worth $500 million are imported annually to control the pest. Africa grows 96 per cent of the 5.4 million tonnes consumed worldwide annually.

To solve the problem, scientists at the Institute for Agricultural Research at Nigeria's Ahmadu Bello University in Zaria have developed a transgenic black-eyed pea variety using insecticide genes from the *Bacillus thuringiensis* bacterium.

Another example is the spread of *Xanthomonas* wilt, a bacterial disease that attacks bananas. It is estimated that the disease costs the [African] Great Lakes region about $500 million annually, predominantly in Uganda. Ugandan researchers are working on a transgenic banana using genes extracted from sweet pepper (*Capsicum annuum*) to control *Xanthomonas*. Ugandan scientists have also developed Golden Bananas with enhanced vitamin A content.

But not all the regions of the world are reaping the full benefits of agricultural biotechnology.

Such new technologies are not silver bullets and need to be integrated into wider socioeconomic systems. Their adoption, however, is currently hampered by restrictive regulations and inefficiencies in Africa's agricultural innovation systems. Much of the teaching in Africa is done in universities that do little research. At the same time, research in carried out in agricultural stations that do not do teaching. The two activities are hardly linked to farmers.

The Need for Innovation

Improving the system will require bringing research, teaching and farm outreach under one roof. A way to achieve this is to create a new generation of agricultural research universities. Such universities need to be part of a wider system of innovation that includes improving interactions between academia, government, business and farmers.

There are two possible ways to help foster agricultural innovation. One is to add research functions to existing agricultural universities and strengthen their linkages to farming communities directly.

The second is to add academic programs to the research activities of the existing national agricultural research institutions (NARIs). Connecting NARIs to farmers in the private sector through extension services and commercialization projects would result in agricultural entrepreneurship.

Creating such institutions will also help maximize the support from new international partnerships seeking to scale up agricultural innovation.

Examples of such partnerships include collaborative efforts of the International Development Research Centre, the Canadian International Development Agency (CIDA) and McGill University to help promote the wider adoption of existing technologies.

Addressing the world's agricultural challenges requires us to rely more on evidence and foresight. As John F. Kennedy noted: "Too often we enjoy the comfort of opinion without the discomfort of thought." We must think ahead.

Genetically Modified Crops Have Not Increased Yield Potential

Institute for Responsible Technology

In the following viewpoint, the Institute for Responsible Technology argues that recent studies show that despite claims to the contrary, genetic modification has not increased crop yields. In fact, the author claims that genetically modified crops have led to crop failure. The Institute for Responsible Technology is an organization that aims to educate policy makers and the public about genetically modified (GM) foods and crops.

As you read, consider the following questions:

1. According to the author, field tests show that genetically modified (GM) corn produced what kind of yields compared with non-GM corn?
2. The author claims that between 1998 and 2004, what percentage of South African genetically modified cotton farmers had given up?
3. The author cites a study by the United Nations Environment Programme (UNEP) that found that farmers using agroecological science outperformed conventional farmers by how much?

From the start, GM [genetically modified] crops have performed no better than their non-GM counterparts. Evidence for the "yield drag" of Roundup Ready soybeans, for example, has been known for over a decade—with the disruptive effect of the GM transformation process accounting for approximately half the drop in yield. Field tests of Bt [*Bacillus thuringiensis*] corn showed that they took longer to reach maturity and produced up to 12% lower yields than non-GM counterparts. In spite of these and other studies, the biotech industry continues to claim that GMOs [genetically modified organisms] are the answer to higher yields. Two reports have conclusively contradicted these claims.

Two Reports on Crop Yields

The International Assessment of Agricultural Knowledge, Science and Technology for Development (IAASTD) report, authored by more than 400 scientists and backed by 58 governments, stated that GM crop yields were "highly variable" and in some cases, "yields declined." The report noted, "Assessment of the technology lags behind its development, information is anecdotal and contradictory, and uncertainty about possible benefits and damage is unavoidable." This assessment was based on a comprehensive evaluation of yield since the introduction of commercial GM crops.

The Union of Concerned Scientists' 2009 report "Failure to Yield" is the definitive study to date on GM crops and yield. Authored by former US Environmental Protection Agency scientist Doug Gurian-Sherman, PhD, it is based on published, peer-reviewed studies conducted by academic scientists using adequate controls. The study concludes that genetically engineering herbicide-tolerant soybeans and herbicide-tolerant corn has not increased yields. Insect-resistant corn has only marginally improved yields. Yield increases of both crops over the last 13 years were largely due to

A Comparison of Crop Yields

[Genetic engineer Jack] Heinemann's group found that between 1985 and 2010, Western Europe has experienced yield gains at a faster rate than North America for all three crops measured. That means that the U.S., which grows mostly GE corn, and Canada, which grows mostly GE canola, are not doing as well as Europe, which grows non-GE corn and canola. The increases in corn yields in the U.S. have remained relatively consistent both before and after the introduction of GE corn. Furthermore, Western Europe is experiencing faster yield gains than America for non-GE wheat.

Jill Richardson, "Research Shows That Monsanto's Big Claims for GMO Food Are Probably Wrong," AlterNet, June 25, 2013.

traditional breeding or improved agricultural practices. Dr. Gurian-Sherman states, "Traditional breeding outperforms genetic engineering hands down."

GM crops have performed no better than their non-GM counterparts.

Although there are few peer-reviewed papers evaluating the yield contribution of GM crops in developing countries, data from Argentina suggest that yields are the same or lower than conventional non-GM soybeans.

The Impact of Crop Failure

In the West, crop failure is often accompanied by government bailouts. Sometimes even seed companies are forced to reimburse farmers, as happened when GM cotton was first grown in the US. Unanticipated plant deformities and failures caused Monsanto to pay farmers millions of dollars for their losses.

In developing countries, crop failure can have severe consequences. This is illustrated in India, where a large number of cotton farmers, unable to pay back high-interest loans, have committed suicide. Several investigations have implicated the unreliable performance of Bt cotton as a major contributor.

Bt cotton was also overrun by pests in Indonesia and China. In South Africa, farmers faced pest problems and no increase in yield. The 100,000 hectares planted in 1998 dropped 80% to 22,500 by 2002. As of 2004, 85% of the original Bt cotton farmers had given up. Those remaining had to be subsidized by the government. Similarly in the US, Bt cotton yields are not necessarily consistent or more profitable.

Assessing the Benefits

It is common for the chemical/biotechnology companies to use conventional or marker-assisted breeding to produce higher yielding crops and afterward cross the variety with a GM crop to add herbicide tolerance or insect resistance. In these cases, higher yields are not due to genetic engineering but to conventional breeding.

There has also been substantial media coverage of supposed GM successes in Africa and elsewhere that never actually materialized. The GM virus-resistant sweet potato, for example, has been a showcase project for Africa, generating significant media coverage. Although Florence Wambugu, the Monsanto-trained scientist, claimed the GM sweet potato doubled output in Kenya, the actual field trial results showed the GM crop to be a failure. By contrast, a conventionally bred, high-yielding, virus-resistant variety in Uganda, developed in less time and at a fraction of the cost, has "raised yields by roughly 100%." Similarly, conventional (non-GM) breeding produced virus-resistant cassavas that do well in Africa even under drought conditions, while the highly promoted GM cassava project has thus far been a failure.

A stunning multiyear study in Africa by the United Nations Environment Programme [UNEP] provides an answer. High external inputs of chemicals and fertilizers are needed for conventional industrial agriculture and it is for this kind of agriculture that GM crops are designed. UNEP found in side-by-side trials conducted in multiple countries that farmers using agroecological science outperformed farmers using conventional approaches by up to 179%. In addition, communities that were in the agroecological trials saw significant improvements in other indicators of food security.

"Organic agriculture has clearly produced increases in food production. Moreover, a switch to organic farming has led to other improvements including environmental improvements, strengthened communities, improvements in the education and health of individuals and a reduction in poverty."

There has also been substantial media coverage of supposed GM successes in Africa and elsewhere that never actually materialized.

The lesson here is that these gains did not require GM plants. In fact, the agricultural industry that promotes GM plants promotes a form of agriculture that is neither sustainable nor conducive to promoting food security and food sovereignty. When asking whether or not to adopt GM, the question is not whether GM has benefits within a non-sustainable agroecosystem such as in the USA, but whether it has benefits when compared to agroecological approaches.

The Arguments Against Genetically Modified Crops Are Invalid

Per Pinstrup-Andersen

In the following viewpoint, Per Pinstrup-Andersen argues that resistance to genetically modified food is resulting in avoidable tragedy. Pinstrup-Andersen claims that the biotechnology has great promise to solve many health, environmental, and food problems worldwide. He claims that the arguments put forth in opposition to genetic modification all are faulty. Pinstrup-Andersen is the H.E. Babcock Professor of Food, Nutrition, and Public Policy at Cornell University.

As you read, consider the following questions:

1. According to the author, for what reason did the Kenyan government not allow genetically modified maize to be grown in their country?

2. For what reason does Pinstrup-Andersen give that the argument against genetically modified food based on a concern about monopoly power fails?

3. What global incident does the author say provides a warning of what the future holds if resistance to genetically modified food continues?

As the world continues to debate the impact of climate change while seeking a new global treaty to prevent it, Kenya has endured a prolonged drought followed by heavy flooding. Maize plants have withered, hitting poor rural families hard. People are starving, and many of those who survive are grossly malnourished.

The Resistance to Genetic Modification

There is hope: Next year, the Kenyan authorities will begin testing maize varieties that they hope will provide high yields and prove more resistant to drought. But why did farmers in Kenya and other African countries not have access to drought-resistant crop varieties before catastrophe struck?

One reason is that such crops rely on research tools used in molecular biology, including genetic engineering. African governments have been told that genetic engineering is dangerous, with many Europeans and their national governments—as well as transnational NGOs [nongovernmental organizations] such as Greenpeace—determined to stay away from it.

Unfortunately, Kenya's government listened and did not permit their farmers to grow genetically modified (GM) maize, even though it has been approved, sown, harvested, and eaten by both humans and animals in South Africa, Argentina, Brazil, the United States, and other countries for many years. Although Kenya has a well-functioning and well-funded agricultural research system, the government has not even permitted field tests of GM crop varieties.

Molecular biology has provided excellent tools to address health, environmental, and food problems such as those seen in Kenya. The question is whether decision makers are prepared to use them. Obviously, most EU [European Union] countries' governments are not. But why are developing-country governments dragging their feet? Are the risks so high that they justify the suffering that could have been avoided?

GM foods have now been on the market in the US for more than 12 years. Most of the food consumed by Americans is either genetically modified or exposed to genetic modification somewhere in the production process. There is no evidence of even a single case of illness or death as a result—in the US or anywhere else where GM foods are consumed. Similarly, GM feed has not resulted in any illness or death in animals. And no environmental damage has been detected.

It is unusual that a new technology has no negative side effects. Just think of all the deaths that the wheel has caused, not to mention the side effects of much of the medicine we take. What, then, is the danger of GM foods?

Molecular biology has provided excellent tools to address health, environmental, and food problems such as those seen in Kenya.

The Arguments Against Genetic Modification

Opponents of genetic engineering in food and agriculture have several arguments, none of which appears to be valid. First, "genetic engineering cannot solve the hunger and food insecurity problem." This is correct: GM foods cannot single-handedly solve the problem, but they can be an important part of the solution.

A second argument is that "we do not know enough about the effects and side effects." Since some of the groups opposing GM organisms destroy the field trials that could give us more knowledge, a more pertinent argument might be that many opponents do not want us to know more.

Third, "we should not play God." But if God gave us brains, it was so that we should use them to ensure a balance between people and nature to help eliminate hunger and protect the environment.

Fourth, pollen from GM crops may "contaminate" organically produced food. This, of course, would be an issue only with open pollinating plants, and only if the definition of "organically produced" excludes GM, something that is difficult to justify, since genes are as organic as anything.

Lastly, some argue that if farmers are permitted to sow GM varieties, they become dependent on large seed producers such as Monsanto, which have patent protection—and thus a monopoly—on the seed. But private corporations undertake only about half of all agricultural research, whether or not it involves genetic engineering. The other half is done by public research systems using public funds. Results from such research would not be subject to private-sector monopoly power. The fact that virtually all US maize and soybean farmers, and all papaya farmers, use GM seed indicates that it is good business for them.

European and developing-country governments urgently need to reverse their current adverse position on GM organisms in order to help ensure sustainable food security for all.

Similarly, a large share of farmers—most of them smallholders—in Argentina, Brazil, South Africa, China, India, and other countries—prefer GM seed because they make more money from the resulting crops. Large reductions in the use of insecticides cut costs for growers of GM varieties, while providing an important health and ecological benefit.

A Damaging Position

But maybe those who oppose private seed corporations are really against capitalism and the market economy rather than GM seed. If so, they should choose an issue for their campaign that would be less damaging to the poor and hungry in developing countries.

The global food crisis of 2007–2008 was a warning of what the future may hold in store if we continue with business as usual, including misplaced opposition to the use of modern science in food and agriculture. European and developing-country governments urgently need to reverse their current adverse position on GM organisms in order to help ensure sustainable food security for all.

Such a reversal would reduce hunger, poverty, and malnutrition; help protect our planet's natural resources; and slow the emission of greenhouse gases from agriculture. All that is needed is political will.

The Arguments Against Genetically Modified Crops Are Based on Science

Peter Melchett

In the following viewpoint, Peter Melchett argues that the campaign to discredit critics of genetic modification based on the charge that such opposition is anti-science fails for several reasons. Melchett contends that not only is opposition to genetically modified food based on science, but he also claims that the proponents of genetic modification fail to adhere to rigorous scientific methods. Melchett is policy director at the Soil Association, a membership charity campaigning for healthy, humane, and sustainable food, farming, and land use in the United Kingdom.

As you read, consider the following questions:

1. Melchett claims that the introduction of genetically modified crops leads to an increase in pesticide use for what reason?
2. According to the author, what does "substantial equivalence" mean in the context of genetically modified crops as used by the Organisation for Economic Co-operation and Development (OECD)?

3. What constitutes the "gold standard" of science, according to the author?

Powerful forces in Western society have been promoting genetic engineering (now usually genetic modification—GM) in agricultural crops since the mid-1990s. They have included many governments, in particular those of the USA and UK [United Kingdom], powerful individual politicians like [former US president] George Bush and [former British prime minister] Tony Blair, scientific bodies like the UK's Royal Society, research councils, successive UK government chief scientists, many individual scientists, and companies selling GM products. They have ignored the views of citizens, and most sales of GM food have relied on secrecy—denying consumers information on what they are buying (20 US states are currently embroiled in fierce battles over GM labelling, strenuously opposed by Monsanto). Worse, they have consistently promoted GM in ways which are not only unscientific, but which have been positively damaging to the integrity of science.

The Anti-Science Charge

This is, of course, an argument usually aimed at those who, like me, are opposed to GM crops. We are accused of being 'anti-science', emotional and irrational, and more recently, of being as bad as 'Nazi book burners' by the president of the National Farmers' Union. This criticism has been effective in framing the debate about GM crops in the media in the UK, where the conflict over GM is routinely presented as a debate between those who are pro and those who are anti-science. This is reinforced by the fact that those selected to speak in favour of GM are usually themselves scientists (albeit often working for GM companies, or funded to work on GM crops), and those selected to oppose GM crops are usually environmentalists, farmers, or citizens concerned about the safety of the food they eat. Scientists who are critical of GM crops are almost never interviewed by the media.

This characterisation of those opposed to GM as being anti-science has always ignored the fact that the NGOs [nongovernmental organisations] concerned, like Greenpeace, Friends of the Earth [International] and the Soil Association, are staunch supporters of science, have scientists working for them, and run campaigns to combat problems which were only identifiable through scientific investigation, like the depletion of the ozone layer and climate change. People opposed to GM, including farmers and environmentalists, often have professional or scientific qualifications, and are well versed in the scientific disciplines that affect agriculture. This has not stopped supporters of GM crops dismissing all of these people as irrational, emotional, anti-science zealots. . . .

The fact that the framing of the debate about the use of GM technology in agriculture, between pro- and anti-science, has been successful does not make it correct.

The fact that the framing of the debate about the use of GM technology in agriculture, between pro- and anti-science, has been successful does not make it correct. In fact, it is those who promote GM crops who have routinely abused science, ignored the basic principles of scientific investigation and proof, and ruthlessly attacked fellow scientists who disagreed with their pro-GM line. In doing so they have misused, abused and devalued science. If people have less respect for science than in the past, I hold the pro-GM lobby partly to blame. They have done real damage to the integrity and independence of science.

Here is the evidence on which I base this accusation.

An Opposition to Products

Pro-GM scientists have made the mistake of conflating their opponents' opposition to commercial products (GM crops) with opposition to science. As I will show, those opposed to

GM crops have a different, and I would say more accurate, understanding of the underlying science. But GM soya seeds are not 'science'—they are a commercial product.

These products have impacts in the real world. For example, they are used to alter the relationship between farmers and seed producers, preventing farmers from saving their own seed. Once a GM variety has been grown, contamination makes it hard for the farmer to revert to non-GM crops, so GM crops tie farmers into long-term relationships with GM seed producers. This allows these companies to exert considerable power over the cost of farmers' inputs (much as multiple retailers do over the price farmers receive for their outputs). It is now clear that existing GM crops have encouraged herbicide-resistant weeds and insecticide-resistant pests. This has led to ever higher use of more complex mixtures of pesticides to control these pests. As a result, the introduction of most GM crops leads to large increases in pesticide use, rather than the decreases predicted by the GM industry.

Pro-GM scientists have made the mistake of conflating their opponents' opposition to commercial products (GM crops) with opposition to science.

The GM traits can be passed by crossing to wild relatives of the crop, and the insecticide in GM Bt [*Bacillus thuringiensis*] crops can destroy beneficial soil fungi. GM crops have negative environmental impacts, as the UK government's scientific research programme (the Farm Scale Evaluations), which I opposed, showed.

To oppose GM crops for all or any of these reasons is not 'anti-science'. On the contrary, opponents of GM use scientific evidence and cite the practical consequences of growing GM crops as arguments against the use of this particular agricultural technology.

An Oversimplified View of Genes

Proponents of GM made the mistake of assuming that the scientific breakthrough of unraveling DNA structure and function, and the discovery of DNA manipulating enzymes (which led to the development of genetic engineering technology being applied to crops), was based on a full understanding of how genes work. As the history of science shows, many great scientific breakthroughs initially appear to have solved some long-standing problem. But on further investigation, it is frequently the case that the new breakthrough raises a host of new questions and areas for investigation. Those of us who love science find this one of the fascinating things about it.

But the companies that were developing GM crops based their ideas on an oversimplistic model of the control of gene expression, and convinced themselves that they were dealing with a straightforward process—hence their initial decision to call the technology of altering crops 'genetic engineering'. They believed that each gene had a single, unique, independent function, and that moving a gene from one plant or animal to another would allow that gene to express that particular function wherever and however it was located.

Even back in the mid-1990s, some scientists said that pro-GM geneticists were oversimplifying gene expression. They pointed out that the geneticists were ignoring relationships that genes have with other genes and relationships that groups of genes have with other groups elsewhere in an organism's DNA. They pointed out too that the geneticists were ignoring the other factors that affect the regulation of gene expression.

We now know that these scientists were right, and that gene expression is more complex than was initially supposed. Gene organisation within the genome is not random. Genes tend to be grouped into coordinated functional units, and control of expression is far more complex than was initially supposed. The emerging science of epigenetics has demonstrated that, for example, mice with identical DNA can turn out to have extreme variations, between disease-prone, obese animals and fit, slim animals, simply because of the impact that dietary inputs and environmental chemical exposures have on their DNA control mechanisms during pregnancy. Much of the scientific case for GM crop technology is based on a grossly oversimplified view—that genes work as isolated units of information—which we now know to be wrong.

One consequence of the disruptive effect of the GM transformation process is that it can negatively affect crop performance (for example 'yield drag' seen with GM soya). Another consequence is the production of novel toxins and allergens, as well as disrupted nutritive value.

The Issue of Substantial Equivalence

Instead of embracing new scientific discoveries in this area, the many scientists involved in promoting GM technology have found a number of ways of trying to disguise or ignore the fact that the processes they are promoting are much more complex than they claim.

For example, transferring genes (usually at random) from one plant to another is a far more uncertain, unstable and disruptive process than was originally thought. In order to avoid the costly and time-consuming safety testing of foods produced through this new technology, the Organisation for Economic Co-operation and Development (OECD)—a body devoted not to public health but to facilitating international trade—came up with the concept of 'substantial equivalence'. This assumes that if relatively simplistic chemical analyses of, say, a GM sweet corn's protein, carbohydrates, vitamins and minerals, find values that can also be found within the range of non-GM sweet corn varieties, then the GM sweet corn is deemed to be indistinguishable from, and therefore as safe as, non-GM sweet corn.

Substantial equivalence was used to deny the need for any biological or toxicological safety testing of GM foods, because GM food was now assumed to be the same as the equivalent food that people had been eating for hundreds of years. This was a political and commercial decision, taken in consultation with, and on behalf of, a small number of large GM companies. It had nothing to do with science. We now know it was opposed by some scientists in the US [Food and] Drug Administration (FDA), but it was pushed through by political appointees to the FDA. The same approach has spread to many other countries, although some are now less enthusiastic, and the European Union avoids using the term "substantial equivalence", redefining it as the "comparative assessment" process. However, proponents of the European concept of "comparative assessment" admit that it has much the same meaning as "substantial equivalence".

An increasing number of detailed biological tests comparing GM and equivalent non-GM crops have now been carried out, not just looking at gross values but rather the spectrum of different types of proteins and other biochemical components. These studies, though few in number, clearly show major differences between the GM and non-GM plants, demonstrating that they are not substantially equivalent. This science invalidates the use of substantial equivalence to assess the safety of GM crops and food, but it is still used in the USA and forms the basis of safety assessments of GM crops in Europe.

Transferring genes (usually at random) from one plant to another is a far more uncertain, unstable and disruptive process than was originally thought.

A Lack of Testing

There is still no requirement, in any country in the world, for GM food to be tested in long-term or lifetime animal feeding trials. Nor is there any requirement to test GM food by feeding it to several generations of mice or rats, to see whether it has any identifiable impact. So there is no regulatory requirement for GM food to be tested to see whether it is safe for humans to eat.

In response, it is claimed that much non-GM plant breeding involves chemical or radiological mutagenesis, and thus gives rise to the same risks as GM crop breeding, so it would be wrong to apply extra controls on GM crops and food. It is true that chemical and radiation-induced mutation crop breeding is highly mutagenic. But there is a good reason why it is not widely used—it produces a large proportion of unhealthy and deformed plants. In fact, some scientists have called for plants produced by mutation breeding to be tested in the same way as GM crops.

In addition, there is the possibility that there are features of the GM process itself that may affect the genome that are not possible in non-GM crop breeding. And GM allows a gene to be inserted in radically different foodstuffs. For example, in the case of allergic reactions, affected individuals could no longer simply avoid foods they know they are allergic to, as GM crop breeding could allow a toxic, allergenic or sensitising protein to be inserted in any food, with no warning labels.

While one result of the adoption of the US interpretation of the unscientific concept of 'substantial equivalence' was to discourage scientific studies of the impact of eating GM foods, in practice, the GM companies try to make sure that studies cannot be conducted at all by independent scientists. As an editorial in *Scientific American* in August 2009 said:

> "It is impossible to verify that genetically modified crops perform as advertised. That is because agritech companies have given themselves veto power over the work of independent researchers. . . . Research on genetically modified seeds is still published, of course. But only studies that the seed

companies have approved ever see the light of a peer-reviewed journal. In a number of cases, experiments that had the implicit go-ahead from the seed company were later blocked from publication because the results were not flattering. . . . It would be chilling enough if any other type of company were able to prevent independent researchers from testing its wares and reporting what they find. . . . But when scientists are prevented from examining the raw ingredients in our nation's food supply or from testing the plant material that covers a large portion of the country's agricultural land, the restrictions on free inquiry become dangerous."

One of the consequences of this determination to stop science working when it comes to research on GM crops, is that numerous pro-GM scientists have fallen into the unscientific trap of claiming that, because GM food has now been eaten by millions of people for several years, it is clearly 'safe'. As most GM food has been eaten in the USA, and in the period since GM food has been produced, the US has suffered a catastrophic increase in diet-related ill health, these same scientists might as well claim that GM food is extraordinarily damaging to human health. Because there has been no GM food labelling in the US, no post-market monitoring, and no epidemiological research, we simply don't know. But to claim that the absence of evidence of harm from GM food means that there is evidence that GM food is safe, when none of the necessary research has been done, shows a willful disregard for basic scientific principles.

There is still no requirement, in any country in the world, for GM food to be tested in long-term or lifetime animal feeding trials.

Although proper studies are difficult to carry out because of the problems of obtaining samples of GM material, some studies have been done looking at the impact of GM diets on animals. Worryingly, these studies, conducted by independent scientists, show negative health effects.

The first and best known of these studies was carried out in Scotland by Dr Árpád Pusztai. His study, and others that have been conducted since, suggest that some adverse impact was being caused to multiple organ systems in the test animals. None of these studies can claim to be conclusive, and most have not been well funded, but they show evidence of potential harm that the scientists involved say needs to be further investigated. All the scientists have been viciously attacked by pro-GM scientists.

Re-evaluations by independent scientists of data obtained from the GM crop industry's own animal feeding studies also demonstrate clear signs of toxicity. The organs consistently affected are the liver and kidney, the two major detoxification organs, with ill effects on the heart, adrenal glands, spleen, and blood cells also being observed.

What is needed are long-term and lifetime animal feeding studies to see the effects of eating GM foods over an extended period—reflecting the real-life exposure of humans. In addition, multigenerational studies are needed to see the effects on reproduction and future generations. Such studies are compulsory for pesticides and pharmaceutical drugs, but not for GM foods—even though the exposure is likely to be longer term for a food than for a pesticide or drug.

One of the great things about science is that, in theory at least, it should not be subject to the whims of those in power or those with money. Anyone making a claim on the basis of scientific evidence should publish their evidence in a form that will allow any other scientist to repeat their experiment, and show whether they are right or wrong. Some of the richest and most powerful organisations in the world attacked Dr Pusztai and his work, particularly the UK's Royal Society. However, to their shame, not one of these critics has seen fit to do what any student learning about scientific method would be told should be the first step, namely, to repeat the experiment. An experiment can be repeated with any modifications that would, in the eyes of the critic, make the study acceptable.

Work done by a young Russian scientist, and by Austrian scientists, has been attacked in exactly the same way, and no effort has been made to repeat those experiments in order to justify these attacks. These personal attacks have sometimes been coupled with threats that the scientists might lose their jobs or funding. But not once anywhere in the world has a pro-GM scientific body or GM company responded to a scientific study they do not like, by doing what anyone who cared about science should do—repeating the experiment.

The Need for Good Science

One response to these criticisms from the pro-GM scientists is to claim that there is in fact a rigorous, scientific, regulatory regime, for example in the USA and EU, which proves that GM crops are safe. The regulatory regime for GM crops is not based on science, but rather on selected information from GM companies. And because of the perceived need for commercial confidentiality, not all the research the companies give to the regulators is published.

The gold standard of science is peer-reviewed, published research. Open publication is fundamental to the integrity of science, and a prerequisite to another key principle on which science rests, namely the fact that conclusions can always be tested by repeating the research. In the area of GM crops, as in some others, what is claimed to be 'scientific' regulation is based on a perversion of science—secretive and (because there is no requirement to publish or even list all studies) possibly highly selective, corporate information.

Independent researchers and NGOs like Greenpeace have used court orders (under EU Freedom of Information laws) to obtain access to previously secret corporate studies. Re-evaluation of the industry raw data shows that the scientists involved selectively studied only a few questions, and interpreted what little evidence they had in ways that favoured corporate interests. Major flaws in the experimental design were evident, which served to mask rather than reveal the effects of the GM transformation process. Nevertheless, these short, 90-day rat feeding studies did show clear signs of toxicity arising from the GM compared to non-GM equivalent feed. If such signs of toxicity are evident after just 90 days, then clearly, lifelong (2-year) studies are urgently needed.

Almost all the claims made for GM crops by proponents of the technology are claims about benefits that GM technology will deliver in the future. This is not a new phenomenon—such claims were being made in the late 1990s, when GM crops were first introduced. Claims that GM crops will solve world hunger, or will deliver drought-resistant, nitrogen-fixing or nutrient-rich crops, are not science but prophecy.

In the area of GM crops . . . what is claimed to be 'scientific' regulation is based on a perversion of science.

The pro-GM lobby and the media treat these claims as if they are science, but none of them are based on scientific evidence. They are opinions, not science, often expressed by companies or scientists with a strong financial interest in seeing them treated as fact. . . .

When the history of the changes in the public understanding of science and public confidence in science over the last fifteen years comes to be written, I believe that the pro-GM lobby's misuse and abuse of science will be seen to have had a chilling impact. These people, organisations and companies have been responsible for part at least of the sad decline in both public understanding and confidence in science and scientific evidence.

Periodical and Internet Sources Bibliography

The following articles have been selected to supplement the diverse views presented in this chapter.

Mariann Bassey	"AGRA's Technology Push in Africa," Friends of the Earth International, 2012.
Jeff Bidstrup	"Who Benefits from GM Crops?," Truth About Trade and Technology, February 20, 2009.
Terra Brockman	"Fooling the World, Not Feeding It," *Zester Daily*, June 16, 2010.
Willy DeGreef	"GM Food for Thought," *European Voice*, November 19, 2009.
Mark Henderson	"Organic Farmers Must Embrace GM Crops If We Are to Feed the World, Says Scientist," *Times* (UK), January 13, 2010.
Eoin Lettice	"We Need GM Plants That Benefit Consumers and Not Just Farmers," *Guardian* (UK), March 9, 2010.
Mark Lynas and Claire Robinson	"Is There a Place for GM Crops in a Sustainable Future?," *New Internationalist*, November 2012.
Robin McKie	"Why the Case for GM Salmon Is Still Hard to Stomach," *Guardian* (UK), August 27, 2010.
Tom Philpott	"Do GMO Crops Really Have Higher Yields?," *Mother Jones*, February 2013.
John Vidal	"GM Crops Promote Superweeds, Food Insecurity, and Pesticides, Say NGOs," *Guardian* (UK), October 19, 2011.
Tom Whipple	"Europe's GM Crops Policy Is Condemned by Farmers," *Times* (UK), July 20, 2013.

**GLOBAL**VIEWPOINTS

CHAPTER 3

The Impact of Genetically Modified Food on Health

Genetically Modified Food May Pose a Real Danger to Health

Ari LeVaux

In the following viewpoint, Ari LeVaux argues that new research has possible ramifications regarding the safety of eating genetically modified food. LeVaux claims that the "central dogma" of genetic science has been shown to be overly simplistic, thus refuting the claim that there is no need for testing the safety of genetically modified food. He contends that more testing is necessary to rule out potential dangers to human health. LeVaux writes Flash in the Pan, a syndicated weekly food column.

As you read, consider the following questions:

1. According to the author, what does the "central dogma" of genetics postulate?
2. The concept of substantial equivalence was developed by what international organization, according to LeVaux?
3. The author suggests what kind of testing be performed, as a start, to test the safety of genetically modified food?

Chinese researchers have found small pieces of rice ribonucleic acid (RNA) in the blood and organs of humans who eat rice. The Nanjing University–based team showed that this genetic material will bind to receptors in human liver cells and influence the uptake of cholesterol from the blood.

The Implications of New Research

The type of RNA in question is called microRNA (abbreviated to miRNA) due to its small size. MiRNAs have been studied extensively since their discovery ten years ago, and have been implicated as players in several human diseases including cancer, Alzheimer's, and diabetes. They usually function by turning down or shutting down certain genes. The Chinese research provides the first *in vivo* [in the living body of a plant or animal] example of ingested plant miRNA surviving digestion and influencing human cell function in this way.

Should the research survive scientific scrutiny—a serious hurdle—it could prove a game changer in many fields. It would mean that we're eating not just vitamins, protein, and fuel, but gene regulators as well.

That knowledge could deepen our understanding of many fields, including cross-species communication, co-evolution, and predator-prey relationships. It could illuminate new mechanisms for some metabolic disorders and perhaps explain how some herbal and modern medicines function.

This study had nothing to do with genetically modified (GM) food, but it could have implications on that front. The work shows a pathway by which new food products, such as GM foods, could influence human health in previously unanticipated ways.

The Central Dogma of Genetics

Monsanto's website states, "There is no need for, or value in testing the safety of GM foods in humans." This viewpoint, while good for business, is built on an understanding of genetics circa 1960. It follows what's called the "Central Dogma" of genetics, which postulates a one-way chain of command between DNA and the cells DNA governs.

The Central Dogma resembles the process of ordering a pizza. The DNA codes for the kind of pizza it wants, and orders it. The RNA is the order slip, which communicates the specifics of that pizza to the cook. The finished and delivered pizza is analogous to the protein that DNA codes for.

This study had nothing to do with genetically modified (GM) food, but it could have implications on that front.

We've known for decades that the Central Dogma, though basically correct, is overly simplistic. For example, miRNAs that don't code for anything, pizza or otherwise, travel within cells silencing genes that are being expressed. So while one piece of DNA is ordering a pizza, it could also be bombarding the pizzeria with RNA signals that can cancel the delivery of other pizzas ordered by other bits of DNA.

Researchers have been using this phenomena to their advantage in the form of small, engineered RNA strands that are virtually identical to miRNA. In a technique called RNA interference, or RNA knockdown, these small bits of RNA are used to turn off, or "knock down," certain genes.

RNA knockdown was first used commercially in 1994 to create the Flavr Savr, a tomato with increased shelf life. In 2007, several research teams began reporting success at engineering plant RNA to kill insect predators, by knocking down certain genes. As reported in MIT's *Technology Review* on November 5, 2007, [by Katherine Bourzac], researchers in China used RNA knockdown to make:

> . . .cotton plants that silence a gene that allows cotton bollworms to process the toxin gossypol, which occurs naturally in cotton. Bollworms that eat the genetically engineered cotton can't make their toxin-processing proteins, and they die.

And:

> Researchers at Monsanto and Devgen, a Belgian company, made corn plants that silence a gene essential for energy production in corn rootworms; ingestion wipes out the worms within 12 days.

The Lack of Testing Requirements

In order to detect health effects caused over time in humans eating GM [genetically modified] foods, long-term (chronic) animal feeding trials are needed. But currently, no long-term tests on GM crops or foods are required by regulatory authorities anywhere in the world. Reproductive and multigenerational tests, which are necessary to discover effects of GM crops or foods on fertility and future generations, are also not required.

This contrasts with the testing requirements for pesticides or drugs, which are far more stringent. Before a pesticide or drug can be approved for use, it must undergo one-year, two-year, and reproductive tests on mammals. Yet GM foods escape such testing, in spite of the fact that virtually all commercialised GM foods are engineered either to contain an insecticide or to tolerate being sprayed with large amounts of herbicide, so they are likely to contain significant amounts of pesticides.

Michael Antoniou, Claire Robinson, and John Fagan,
"GMO Myths and Truths: An Evidence-Based Examination
of the Claims Made for the Safety and Efficacy of
Genetically Engineered Crops," Earth Open Source, June 2012.

Humans and insects have a lot in common, genetically. If miRNA can in fact survive the gut then it's entirely possible that miRNA intended to influence insect gene regulation could also affect humans.

The Doctrine of Substantial Equivalence

Monsanto's claim that human toxicology tests are unwarranted is based on the doctrine of "substantial equivalence." According to substantial equivalence, comparisons between

GM and non-GM crops need only investigate the end products of DNA expression. New DNA is not considered a threat in any other way.

"So long as the introduced protein is determined to be safe, food from GM crops determined to be substantially equivalent is not expected to pose any health risks," reads Monsanto's website.

In other words, as long as the final product—the pizza, as it were—is nontoxic, the introduced DNA isn't any different and doesn't pose a problem. For what it's worth, if that principle were applied to intellectual property law, many of Monsanto's patents would probably be null and void.

Chen-Yu Zhang, the lead researcher on the Chinese RNA study, has made no comment regarding the implications of his work for the debate over the safety of GM food. Nonetheless, these discoveries help give shape to concerns about substantial equivalence that have been raised for years from within the scientific community.

Monsanto's claim that human toxicology tests are unwarranted is based on the doctrine of "substantial equivalence."

In 1999, a group of scientists wrote a letter titled "Beyond 'Substantial Equivalence'" to the prestigious journal *Nature*. In the letter, Erik Millstone *et al.* called substantial equivalence "a pseudo-scientific concept" that is "inherently anti-scientific because it was created primarily to provide an excuse for not requiring biochemical or toxicological tests."

To these charges, Monsanto responded: "The concept of substantial equivalence was elaborated by international scientific and regulatory experts convened by the Organisation for Economic Co-operation and Development (OECD) in 1991, well before any biotechnology products were ready for market."

This response is less a rebuttal than a testimonial to Monsanto's prowess at handling regulatory affairs. Of course the term was established before any products were ready for the market. Doing so was a prerequisite to the global commercialization of GM crops. It created a legal framework for selling GM foods anywhere in the world that substantial equivalence was accepted. By the time substantial equivalence was adopted, Monsanto had already developed numerous GM crops and was actively grooming them for market.

The OECD's 34 member nations could be described as largely rich, white, developed, and sympathetic to big business. The group's current mission is to spread economic development to the rest of the world. And while the mission has yet to be accomplished, OECD has helped Monsanto spread substantial equivalence globally.

The Need for More Testing

Many GM fans will point out that if we do toxicity tests on GM foods, we should also have to do toxicity testing on every other kind of food in the world.

But we've already done the testing on the existing plants. We tested them the hard way, by eating strange things and dying, or almost dying, over thousands of years. That's how we've figured out which plants are poisonous. And over the course of each of our lifetimes we've learned which foods we're allergic to.

All of the non-GM breeds and hybrid species that we eat have been shaped by the genetic variability offered by parents whose genes were similar enough that they could mate, graft, or test tube baby their way to an offspring that resembled them.

A tomato with fish genes? Not so much. That, to me, is a new plant and it should be tested. We shouldn't have to figure out if it's poisonous or allergenic the old-fashioned way, especially in light of how newfangled the science is.

It's time to rewrite the rules to acknowledge how much more complicated genetic systems are than the legal regulations—and the corporations that have written them—give credit.

The Resistance to Testing

Monsanto isn't doing itself any PR favors by claiming "no need for, or value in testing the safety of GM foods in humans." Admittedly, such testing can be difficult to construct—who really wants to volunteer to eat a bunch of GM corn just to see what happens? At the same time, if companies like Monsanto want to use processes like RNA interference to make plants that can kill insects via genetic pathways that might resemble our own, some kind of testing has to happen.

It's time for Monsanto to acknowledge that there's more to DNA than the proteins it codes for.

A good place to start would be the testing of introduced DNA for other effects—miRNA-mediated or otherwise—beyond the specific proteins they code for. But the status quo, according to Monsanto's website, is:

> There is no need to test the safety of DNA introduced into GM crops. DNA (and resulting RNA) is present in almost all foods. DNA is nontoxic and the presence of DNA, in and of itself, presents no hazard.

Given what we know, that stance is arrogant. Time will tell if it's reckless.

There are computational methods of investigating whether unintended RNAs are likely to be knocking down any human genes. But thanks to this position, the best we can do is hope they're using them. Given its opposition to the labeling of GM foods as well, it seems clear that Monsanto wants you to close your eyes, open your mouth, and swallow.

It's time for Monsanto to acknowledge that there's more to DNA than the proteins it codes for—even if it's for no other reason than the fact that RNA alone is a lot more complicated than [molecular biologists James] Watson and [Francis] Crick could ever have imagined.

Studies Worldwide Show Genetically Modified Food Is Safe

Ramez Naam

In the following viewpoint, Ramez Naam argues that there is a scientific consensus worldwide about the safety of genetically modified food. Naam quotes several scientific bodies, medical associations, and judicial entities as finding the research in favor of the safety of consuming food that has genetically modified ingredients. He contends that the few studies that argue otherwise are not credible. Naam is author of The Infinite Resource: The Power of Ideas on a Finite Planet *and* More than Human: Embracing the Promise of Biological Enhancement.

As you read, consider the following questions:

1. According to the author, what is the opinion of the American Medical Association regarding the safety of eating genetically modified food?

2. What does England's Royal Society of Medicine say about the safety of genetically modified food, according to Naam?

3. What three problems does the author claim scientists have found with the studies that say genetically modified foods harm animals?

I was on the Melissa Harris-Perry show today, speaking about GMOs [genetically modified organisms]. . . .

First, a statement on my interests: I have no relationship whatsoever with Monsanto or any other ag [agriculture] or biotech company. I hold no Monsanto stock. I get no money from them. Nothing of the sort. My only interest is in advancing public knowledge of a technology that's widely misunderstood and which, when well managed, can benefit both humanity and the planet. All the research I presented was research I did when writing my book on innovating to save the planet, *The Infinite Resource: The Power of Ideas on a Finite Planet.*

I do believe that we'll eventually have labels on genetically modified foods. So long as those labels are in the ingredients section and not needlessly frightening, I think that's fine. Clearly a set of people very much want labels, and the resistance to labeling gives the appearance that there's something to hide with genetically modified foods. There isn't. Genetically modified foods are safe.

Because there wasn't enough time to go into detail on the show, I want to link to statements from the world's most respected scientific bodies and journals on the topic of GMO safety. Here's what they say.

Genetically modified foods are safe.

Statements from the United States

US National Academy of Sciences

This is the premier scientific body in the United States. They have repeatedly found genetically modified food safe, noting that after billions of meals served, "no adverse health effects attributed to genetic engineering have been documented in the human population."

They've also found that genetically engineered crops are *kinder* to the environment than non–genetically engineered crops. The National Academy of Sciences' 2010 report, "The Impact of Genetically Engineered Crops on Farm Sustainability in the United States," found that GM crops planted to date had *reduced* insecticide use, *reduced* use of the most dangerous herbicides, increased the frequency of conservation tillage and no-till farming, reduced carbon emissions, reduced soil run-offs, and improved soil quality. The report said that, "Generally, GE (GMO) crops have had fewer adverse effects on the environment than non-GE crops produced conventionally."

American Association for the Advancement of Science [AAAS]

This is the largest organization made up of professional scientists in the United States, and also publisher of *Science* magazine, one of the two most respected scientific journals in the world. The AAAS says, "The science is quite clear: crop improvement by the modern molecular techniques of biotechnology is safe."

American Medical Association

The premier body of physicians in the United States. They have consistently found genetically modified foods as safe to eat as any other food, stating "there is no scientific justification for special labeling of genetically modified foods."

Statements from Europe

European Commission

Europe is extremely anti-GMO. But even there, the scientific community is clear that genetically modified foods are safe. The scientific advisor to the European Commission has said "there is no more risk in eating GMO food than eating conventionally farmed food."

The European Commission's 2010 report on genetically engineered food (based on independent research not funded by any biotech company) said: "The main conclusion to be

---

The Critics of Genetically Modified Food

The critics of genetic engineering in agriculture—also known as "genetic modification" (GM) or gene splicing—for decades have relied upon and promulgated The Big Lie: that food from genetically engineered crops is untested, unsafe, unwanted, and unneeded. All of these assertions, made by radical anti-technology organizations such as the National Resources Defense Council (NRDC), Environmental Defense [aka Environmental Defense Fund], the Center for Science in the Public Interest, the Center for Food Safety, the Union of Concerned Scientists, and Greenpeace are demonstrably false.

Henry I. Miller, "Organic Is Overrated,"
Defining Ideas, *July 26, 2012.*

---

drawn from the efforts of more than 130 research projects, covering a period of more than 25 years of research, and involving more than 500 independent research groups, is that biotechnology, and in particular GMOs, are not per se more risky than e.g. conventional plant breeding technologies."

Royal Society of Medicine

England's top medical society, the equivalent of the United States' American Medical Association, published a review of all the information about genetically modified foods that concluded, "Foods derived from GM crops have been consumed by hundreds of millions of people across the world for more than 15 years, with no reported ill effects (or legal cases related to human health), despite many of the consumers coming from that most litigious of countries, the USA."

French Supreme Court

The French Supreme Court isn't a scientific body, but I mention them here because their recent decision was so remarkable. France is a very anti-GMO country. Yet the French Supreme Court struck down France's GMO ban, ruling that the government had shown no credible evidence of any harm to humans or the environment. . . .

A Few Non-Credible Studies

Thus far there have been several hundred studies on the safety of genetically engineered food. All but a handful have found them completely safe. The only studies that have found that genetically modified foods harm animals (the ones quoted as saying that they cause cancer and infertility) all come from one laboratory, that of Gilles-Éric Séralini in France.

Yet Séralini's studies have been widely debunked.

All together, the scientific consensus around the safety of genetically modified foods is as strong as the scientific consensus around climate change.

And even food advocates find them hard to believe. My fellow guest on MSNBC, food policy advocate (and GMO labeling proponent) Marion Nestle, herself has said that she finds them hard to believe. Marion Nestle writes:

These results are so graphically shocking, and so discrepant from previous studies, that they bring out my skeptical tendencies. (Note: Although Séralini is apparently a well-known opponent of GMOs, his study—and that of the review—were funded by government or other independent agencies.) . . . The study is weirdly complicated.

And respectable scientists writing in the journal *Nature* (the other most respected scientific journal in the world, along with *Science*) found numerous problems with the GMO-rat-cancer study. Among other things, Séralini (the scientist claiming that GMOs cause cancer) refused to let science journalists see the paper ahead of the press release, found something that other researchers doing very similar studies have never found, and refused to share the actual data of [his] experiments.

All together, the scientific consensus around the safety of genetically modified food is as strong as the scientific consensus around climate change. These foods have been studied more than any other, and everything tells us that they're safe.

In Australia, Food Industry Specialists Fear Genetically Modified Wheat Would Be Harmful for Health

Neil Perry and Martin Boetz

In the following viewpoint, Neil Perry and Martin Boetz argue that genetically modified wheat should not be introduced in Australia. Perry and Boetz contend that there is no evidence that genetically modified wheat is safe. They conclude that to promote health, Australia should stick with encouraging a good traditional diet rather than spending money and time on an untested, new food. Perry is owner of several restaurants, and Boetz is owner and executive chef of several restaurants in Australia.

As you read, consider the following questions:

1. According to the authors, what unhealthy foods do big manufacturers currently promote in Australia?
2. Perry and Boetz claim that proponents of genetically modified wheat claim that it could help reduce rates of what disease?
3. Instead of spending money creating genetically modified products, the authors suggest that to promote health society should follow what advice?

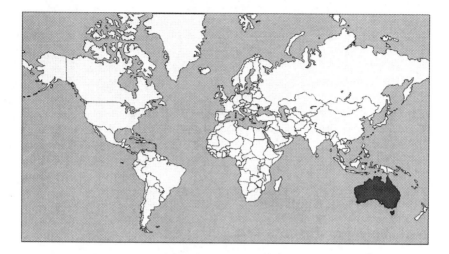

We are proud to be two of Australia's leading chefs and food industry spokesmen. Making and serving fresh and tasty food is a great pleasure for us. We have built our lives and careers around this passion.

The Integrity of Food

But we are disturbed by the prospect that Australia may become one of the first countries in the world to grow and eat genetically modified [GM] wheat. Wheat is a fundamental part of our daily diet, the basis of bread, pasta, noodles, pastries and many other foods.

Whether or not you agree with its methods, Greenpeace's destruction of GM wheat from a CSIRO [Commonwealth Scientific and Industrial Research Organisation] trial site just outside Canberra last week [July 14, 2011] has stirred up the debate. And the state of our food—and the ways it is produced—is a debate worth having.

The integrity of our food is continually being depleted by the demands of a fast-paced modern lifestyle. Our relationship with food is generally an unhealthy one. Agri-food manufacturers play on people's time poverty to sell ultra-processed fast foods full of salt, sugar, highly refined carbohydrates, additives and preservatives. These foods have nothing in common with the fresh fruit and vegetables and whole cereals that should make up the bulk of a healthy diet.

The Argument for GM Wheat

The CSIRO claims its experimental GM wheat could help reduce bowel cancer rates because of more "resistant starch", which is good for digestive health. Encouraging people to eat more brown bread, rice and oats would seem eminently safer and more sensible and affordable. And this can be done without turning to GM crops, which we consider to be unsafe. But of course that's not attractive to big international biotech firms that see a commercial advantage in GM crops.

The CSIRO and the Australian government are contradicting their own health advice that people should eat more whole grains and a more varied diet. If people carry on eating the same kind of processed foods, drained of all the nutrients and life-giving energy we need, we can expect health problems to continue. GM wheat won't help this; the likelihood is it will only increase the amount of unnatural, processed food on supermarket shelves.

Even more troubling is the fact that GM plants have never been proven safe to eat. Through trial and error over many thousands of years, we have found what we can eat for health and nourishment and what we must stay away from.

New forms of food such as GM wheat have never been tested for safety. They have not undergone the kind of trial and error that all our naturally occurring foods have over thousands of years of being consumed—they are a whole new form of genetically modified life. And they have not been through the kind of safety testing demanded of new pharmaceutical products.

The Need to Protect Australia's Food

Food is a fundamental part of life. Protecting the integrity of our food and the reliability of our food supply is critical. We must ask what kind of world we are building for ourselves and for our children where we would prefer to spend billions of dollars creating unnecessary and risky genetically modified products, rather than following our grandmothers' and mothers' advice of simply eating a balanced diet.

In a few generations our food and farming systems have been radically transformed. Once based around nature and human need, they are now controlled by corporations, from seed to supermarket, for the purpose of profit.

We are urging the Australian government to stop risking Australia's food industry and to put a stop to GM wheat trials.

The menus in our restaurants, like those of other restaurants, cafes and family kitchens all around the country, feature wheat products such as bread and pastry every day. GM wheat will jeopardise our capacity to serve wholesome food we can rely on.

As leading chefs in Australia, we will stop using wheat products if GM becomes prevalent, or we will exclusively use certified organic wheat.

Australia's reputation as one of the best food producers and places to eat in the world is at risk. We are urging the Australian government to stop risking Australia's food industry and to put a stop to GM wheat trials.

In the Philippines and Elsewhere, Genetically Modified Rice Can Prevent Disease

Bjørn Lomborg

In the following viewpoint, Bjørn Lomborg argues that vitamin A deficiency kills or blinds hundreds of thousands of people each year, but genetically modified rice can solve the problem effectively and inexpensively. Lomborg claims that opposition to Golden Rice is unscientific and is costing people their lives. Lomborg is founder and director of the Copenhagen Consensus Center, adjunct professor at the Copenhagen Business School, and author of The Skeptical Environmentalist.

As you read, consider the following questions:

1. The author cites an estimate finding that how many children under the age of five die each year from vitamin A deficiency?

2. According to Lomborg, how much less expensive is it to save a life from vitamin A deficiency with Golden Rice than with supplementation or fortification?

3. How many children in the Philippines have vitamin A deficiency that can be helped by eating Golden Rice, according to Lomborg?

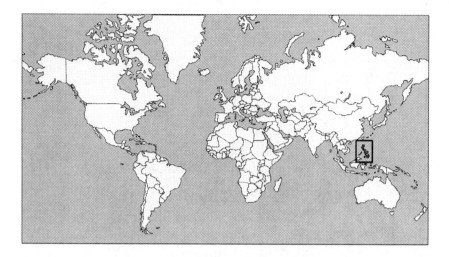

Finally, after 12 years of delay caused by opponents of genetically modified (GM) foods, so-called "Golden Rice" with vitamin A will be grown in the Philippines. Over those 12 years, about eight million children worldwide died from vitamin A deficiency. Are anti-GM advocates not partly responsible?

The Controversy About Golden Rice

Golden Rice is the most prominent example in the global controversy over GM foods, which pits a technology with some risks but incredible potential against the resistance of feel-good campaigning. Three billion people depend on rice as their staple food, with 10% at risk for vitamin A deficiency, which, according to the World Health Organization, causes 250,000–500,000 children to go blind each year. Of these, half die within a year. A study from the British medical journal the *Lancet* estimates that, in total, vitamin A deficiency kills 668,000 children under the age of five each year.

Yet, despite the cost in human lives, anti-GM campaigners—from Greenpeace to [Canadian social activist] Naomi Klein—have derided efforts to use Golden Rice to avoid vitamin A deficiency. In India, Vandana Shiva, an environmental activist and adviser to the government, called Golden Rice "a hoax" that is "creating hunger and malnutrition, not solving it."

The *New York Times Magazine* reported in 2001 that one would need to "eat 15 pounds of cooked Golden Rice a day" to get enough vitamin A. What was an exaggeration then is demonstrably wrong now. Two recent studies in the *American Journal of Clinical Nutrition* show that just 50 grams (roughly two ounces) of Golden Rice can provide 60% of the recommended daily intake of vitamin A. They show that Golden Rice is even better than spinach in providing vitamin A to children.

Golden Rice is the most prominent example in the global controversy over GM foods.

The Opposition to Golden Rice

Opponents maintain that there are better ways to deal with vitamin A deficiency. In its latest statement, Greenpeace says that Golden Rice is "neither needed nor necessary," and calls instead for supplementation and fortification, which are described as "cost-effective."

To be sure, handing out vitamin pills or adding vitamin A to staple products can make a difference. But it is not a sustainable solution to vitamin A deficiency. And, while it is cost-effective, recently published estimates indicate that Golden Rice is much more so.

Supplementation programs cost $4,300 for every life they save in India, whereas fortification programs cost about $2,700 for each life saved. Both are great deals. But Golden Rice would cost just $100 for every life saved from vitamin A deficiency.

Similarly, it is argued that Golden Rice will not be adopted, because most Asians eschew brown rice. But brown rice is

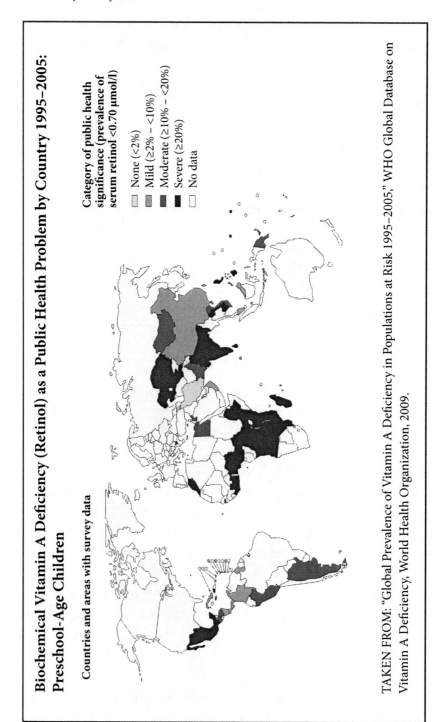

Biochemical Vitamin A Deficiency (Retinol) as a Public Health Problem by Country 1995–2005: Preschool-Age Children

Countries and areas with survey data

Category of public health significance (prevalence of serum retinol <0.70 μmol/l)

- None (<2%)
- Mild (≥2% – <10%)
- Moderate (≥10% – <20%)
- Severe (≥20%)
- No data

TAKEN FROM: "Global Prevalence of Vitamin A Deficiency in Populations at Risk 1995–2005," WHO Global Database on Vitamin A Deficiency, World Health Organization, 2009.

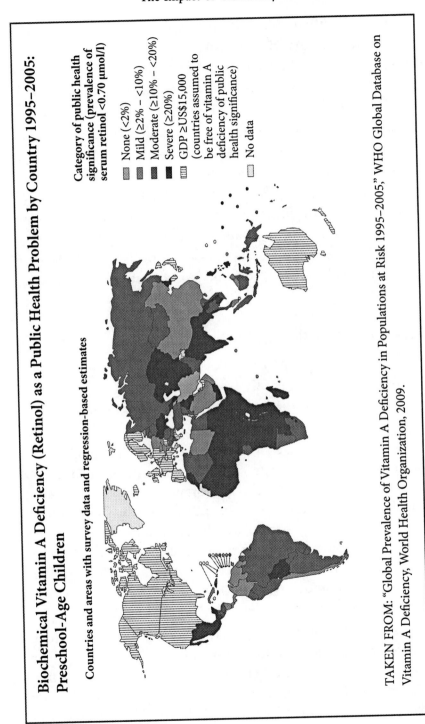

Biochemical Vitamin A Deficiency (Retinol) as a Public Health Problem by Country 1995–2005: Preschool-Age Children

Countries and areas with survey data and regression-based estimates

Category of public health significance (prevalence of serum retinol <0.70 μmol/l)

- None (<2%)
- Mild (≥2% – <10%)
- Moderate (≥10% – <20%)
- Severe (≥20%)
- GDP ≥US$15,000 (countries assumed to be free of vitamin A deficiency of public health significance)
- No data

TAKEN FROM: "Global Prevalence of Vitamin A Deficiency in Populations at Risk 1995–2005," WHO Global Database on Vitamin A Deficiency, World Health Organization, 2009.

substantially different in taste and spoils easily in hot climates. Moreover, many Asian dishes are already colored yellow with saffron, annatto, achiote, and turmeric. The people, not Greenpeace, should decide whether they will adopt vitamin A–rich rice for themselves and their children.

Most ironic is the self-fulfilling critique that many activists now use. Greenpeace calls Golden Rice a "failure," because it "has been in development for almost 20 years and has still not made any impact on the prevalence of vitamin A deficiency." But, as Ingo Potrykus, the scientist who developed Golden Rice, has made clear, that failure is due almost entirely to relentless opposition to GM foods—often by rich, well-meaning Westerners far removed from the risks of actual vitamin A deficiency.

The Impact of Regulation

Regulation of goods and services for public health clearly is a good idea; but it must always be balanced against potential costs—in this case, the cost of not providing more vitamin A to eight million children over the past 12 years.

As an illustration, current regulations for GM foods, if applied to non-GM products, would bar the sale of potatoes and tomatoes, which can contain poisonous glycoalkaloids; celery, which contains carcinogenic psoralens; rhubarb and spinach (oxalic acid); and cassava, which feeds about half a billion people, but contains toxic cyanogenic alkaloids. Foodstuffs like soy, wheat, milk, eggs, mollusks, crustaceans, fish, sesame, nuts, peanuts, and kiwi would likewise be banned, because they can cause food allergies.

Here it is worth noting that there have been no documented human health effects from GM foods. But many campaigners have claimed other effects. A common story, still repeated by Shiva, is that GM corn with Bt [*Bacillus thuringiensis*] toxin kills Monarch butterflies. Several peer-reviewed studies, however, have effectively established that "the impact of Bt corn pollen from current commercial hybrids on Monarch butterfly populations is negligible."

Regulation of goods and services for public health clearly is a good idea; but it must always be balanced against potential costs.

Greenpeace and many others claim that GM foods merely enable big companies like Monsanto to wield near monopoly power. But that puts the cart before the horse: The predominance of big companies partly reflects anti-GM activism, which has made the approval process so long and costly that only rich companies catering to first world farmers can afford to see it through.

The Need for Perspective

Finally, it is often claimed that GM crops simply mean costlier seeds and less money for farmers. But farmers have a choice. More than five million cotton farmers in India have flocked to GM cotton, because it yields higher net incomes. Yes, the seeds are more expensive, but the rise in production offsets the additional cost.

Of course, no technology is without flaws, so regulatory oversight is useful. But it is worth maintaining some perspective. In 2010, the European Commission, after considering 25 years of GM organisms (GMOs) research, concluded that "there is, as of today, no scientific evidence associating GMOs with higher risks for the environment or for food and feed safety than conventional plants and organisms."

Now, finally, Golden Rice will come to the Philippines; after that, it is expected in Bangladesh and Indonesia. But, for eight million kids, the wait was too long.

True to form, Greenpeace is already protesting that "the next 'Golden Rice' guinea pigs might be Filipino children." The 4.4 million Filipino kids with vitamin A deficiency might not mind so much.

The World Needs Genetically Modified Food to End Hunger

Robert Paarlberg

In the following viewpoint, Robert Paarlberg argues that the unscientific resistance to genetically modified food is a luxury in rich nations that will have ill effects on poor nations. Paarlberg contends that many genetically modified products are not making it to the marketplace because of unjustified mistrust, when such products could address health and hunger issues in nations worldwide. Paarlberg is a professor of political science at Wellesley College and associate at the Weatherhead Center for International Affairs at Harvard University.

As you read, consider the following questions:

1. According to Paarlberg, for what reason does the US Food and Drug Administration oppose the mandatory labeling of genetically modified food?

2. Why did food service chains say they did not want genetically modified potatoes, according to the author?

3. In what way would East Africa be helped by the introduction of genetically modified maize, according to Paarlberg?

The Whole Foods grocery chain recently announced its intent by 2018 to require labels on all foods with genetically engineered ingredients. This step was hailed as a game changer by those campaigning to make such labels a federal requirement. Yet even without mandatory labeling, most genetically modified [organism] (or GMO) foods have already been driven out of our supermarkets.

A Lack of Risk

People in wealthy countries can afford to live with this outcome. But in the long run, it will take important choices away from farmers and consumers in poor countries.

The U.S. Food and Drug Administration has long opposed the mandatory labeling of GMO foods because it agrees with a scientific consensus that these foods so far bring no new risks to human health or the environment. All of the leading national science academies in Europe have reached this conclusion. Three years ago, the research directorate of the European Union concluded that biotechnology, and in particular GMOs, "are not per se more risky than, for example, conventional plant breeding technologies."

Most genetically modified . . . foods have already been driven out of our supermarkets.

Nonetheless, campaigns by activist groups such as Greenpeace have so scared consumers that most GMO food products have been kept out of the American marketplace.

Products Kept Out of the Marketplace

A genetically modified wheat designed to reduce the cost of weed control was first field-tested in 1994, but in 2004 Monsanto decided not to go ahead with sales of wheat seeds when it became clear that American and Canadian farmers feared consumer resistance and lost export sales in Europe and Asia.

GMO rice that can be grown with less pesticide spray has been field-tested in the U.S. since 1990—but, for similar reasons, never commercialized. GMO potatoes that resist beetle damage were grown successfully in the U.S. from 1999 to 2001, but their cultivation was voluntarily suspended when food service chains told farmers that they didn't want to be accused by activists of selling GMO French fries.

GMO tomatoes with a convenient trait that delays ripening were grown between 1998 and 2002, but cultivation was then suspended. GMO melons capable of resisting a virus have been successfully tested in the U.S. since 1989 but never planted commercially.

Developing countries have significant unmet food needs, and GMO food crops are positioned to help.

It is often reported that roughly 70% of foods in the U.S. contain some ingredients from genetically engineered crops, but most of those ingredients are by-products such as oil, starch or sweeteners derived from just three GMO crops: soybeans, corn and sugar beets. If the U.S. enacted a mandatory labeling law, the impacts might be surprisingly small. To avoid the stigmatizing labels, food companies could reformulate many of their products, for example by turning to oil from non-GMO corn and soy, or by using non-GMO palm or sunflower oil. By-products from GMO corn and soy could then be diverted to industrial or biofuel use.

America's farmers might also find an acceptable workaround. Currently 98% of their soy and 88% of their corn is already employed as feedstock for biofuels or as animal feed, neither of which requires a label. But there would be a large downside in poor countries for moving further along this path.

A Setback for the Poor and Hungry

Developing countries have significant unmet food needs, and GMO food crops are positioned to help. In Asia, poor consumers who currently don't get enough vitamin A from their rice-only diets could be better protected against blindness if their farmers had permission to plant so-called Golden Rice, which has been genetically engineered with high beta-carotene content.

Farmers and consumers in India currently exposed to toxic insecticides when they grow and eat eggplant could reduce their exposure if farmers had access to a GMO eggplant, Bt [*Bacillus thuringiensis*] brinjal, that needs fewer chemical sprays. Farmers and consumers in East Africa currently vulnerable to hunger and destitution when drought hits their maize fields would be more secure if growers had permission to plant GMO drought-resistant varieties of white maize.

But if America, through a labeling system, joins Europe in embracing a new norm against the cultivation of GMO crops for human food, governments in developing countries, already skittish thanks to activist campaigns, will likely follow suit. The result would be a needless setback for the world's poorest and hungriest people.

In Africa, Genetically Modified Food Has Failed to Help End World Hunger

Michael Antoniou, Claire Robinson, and John Fagan

In the following viewpoint, Michael Antoniou, Claire Robinson, and John Fagan argue that genetically modified food is not the answer to world hunger. They contend that the failure of several genetically modified crops in Africa illustrates that the biotechnology does not increase yields or save farmers money. Furthermore, they say that the real source of world hunger has nothing to do with a lack of food, but with access to it. Antoniou is head of the Nuclear Biology Group at King's College London; Robinson is research director at Earth Open Source; and Fagan is director at Earth Open Source.

As you read, consider the following questions:

1. According to the authors, the two major genetically modified crops of soy and maize cannot meet basic food needs because they are used for what?
2. What are three of the negative effects the authors claim resulted from a genetically modified soy and maize project in South Africa?
3. The authors claim that the World Bank and the United Nations Food and Agriculture Organization identified what as the main cause of the 2007–2008 food crisis?

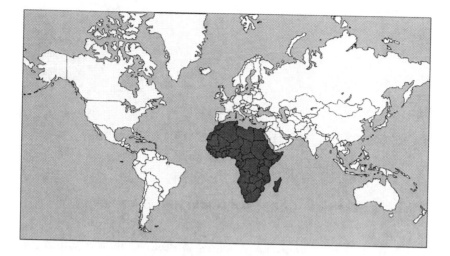

G M [genetically modified] crops are promoted as a way of solving world hunger at a time when the population is expected to increase. But it is difficult to see how GM can contribute to solving world hunger when there are no GM crops available that increase intrinsic yield. Nor are there any GM crops that are better than non-GM crops at tolerating poor soils or challenging climate conditions.

Hunger and Genetic Modification

Instead, most currently available GM crops are engineered for herbicide tolerance or to contain a pesticide, or both. The two major GM crops, soy and maize, mostly go into animal feed, biofuels to power cars, and processed human food—products for developed nations that have nothing to do with meeting the basic food needs of the poor and hungry. GM corporations are answerable to their shareholders and thus are interested in profitable commodity markets, not in feeding the poor and hungry.

Even if a GM crop did appear that gave higher yields than non-GM crops, this would not impact the problem of hunger. This is because the root cause of hunger is not a lack of food, but a lack of access to food. According to the UN [United Nations] Food and Agriculture Organization, we already produce more than enough food to feed the world's population and could produce enough with existing agricultural methods to feed 12 billion people. The problem is that the poor have no money to buy food and increasingly, no access to land on which to grow it. Hunger is a social, political, and economic problem, which GM technology cannot address. GM is a dangerous distraction from real solutions and claims that GM can help feed the world can be viewed as exploitation of the suffering of the hungry.

It is difficult to see how GM can contribute to solving world hunger when there are no GM crops available that increase intrinsic yield.

A handful of GM crops have been promoted as helping small-scale and poor farmers in Africa. However, the results were the opposite of what was promised.

The GM Sweet Potato

The virus-resistant sweet potato has been a GM showcase project for Africa, generating global media coverage. Florence Wambugu, the Monsanto-trained scientist fronting the project, has been proclaimed an African heroine and the saviour of millions, based on her claims that the GM sweet potato doubled output in Kenya. *Forbes* magazine even declared her one of a tiny handful of people around the globe who would "reinvent the future".

But it eventually emerged that the claims being made for the GM sweet potato were untrue, with field trial results showing it to be a failure. The GM sweet potato was outyielded by the non-GM control and succumbed to the virus it was designed to resist.

In contrast, a conventional breeding programme in Uganda produced a new high-yielding variety that was virus resistant and raised yields by roughly 100%. The Ugandan project achieved its goal in a fraction of the time and cost of the GM project. The GM sweet potato project, over 12 years, consumed funding from Monsanto, the World Bank, and USAID [United States Agency for International Development] to the tune of $6 million.

The GM Cassava

The potential of genetic engineering to boost the production of cassava—one of Africa's staple foods—by defeating a devastating virus has been heavily promoted since the mid-1990s. It was even claimed that GM cassava could solve hunger in Africa by increasing yields as much as tenfold.

But almost nothing appears to have been achieved. Even after it became clear that the GM cassava had suffered a major technical failure, losing resistance to the virus, media stories continued to appear about its curing hunger in Africa.

Meanwhile, conventional (non-GM) plant breeding has quietly produced a virus-resistant cassava that is already proving successful in farmers' fields, even under drought conditions. . . .

GM Soy and Maize

A GM soy and maize farming project ended in disaster for poor black farmers in South Africa. The Eastern Cape government was criticised for its support of this so-called "Green Revolution" project, which was launched in 2003–2004. A research study by the Masifunde Education and Development Project Trust, together with Rhodes University, found that the programme had disastrous results for farmers.

"We saw a deepening of poverty and people returning to the land for survival," said Masifunde researcher Mercia Andrews. The study raised concerns about feeding schemes conducted on animals with "alarming results", including damage to internal organs. It presented evidence of weed and pest problems, contamination of crops with GM pollen, and the control exercised by big companies over local and global food systems as a result of patented seeds.

We conclude from these examples that it is irresponsible to pressure poor farmers in the Global South into gambling their farms and livelihoods on risky GM crops when proven effective alternatives exist. . . .

The Global Food Crisis

The 2007–2008 global food crisis led to food riots around the world, as the escalating price of staple crops pushed food out of reach of the poor and hungry. The crisis is ongoing—in early 2011 global food prices remained close to their 2008 peak. They declined 8% between September and December 2011, though the World Bank reported that they were still high, with the 2011 annual food price index exceeding the 2010 annual index by 24%.

GM proponents have used the food crisis to claim that anti-GM activists in the Global North are keeping the Global South hungry by creating unfounded fears about GM crops. These high-technology GM crops, they claimed, could help solve the hunger problem, if only the activists in affluent countries would stop interfering. But the World Bank and the United Nations Food and Agriculture Organization identified the biofuels boom—not a lack of GM foods—as the main cause of the 2007–2008 food crisis.

The biofuels boom has coupled food prices to fossil fuel prices, with the result that food prices will continue to spiral as petroleum becomes scarcer and more expensive.

Biofuels are crops used for fuel. Vast tracts of cropland have been taken out of food production to grow biofuels for cars, funded by generous government subsidies. This has made food scarcer, pushing up costs.

An added factor is that the growth of the biofuels industry has created a link between agriculture and fuel that never existed before.

Previously, agricultural markets were driven only by food demands and were not linked to petroleum markets. But now they are tightly linked, because agriculture provides the crops that are used to make the biofuels alternative to petrochemical fuels. Four major food and feed crops—sugarcane, maize, wheat, and soy—are now used for biofuels feedstock. So the biofuels boom has coupled food prices to fossil fuel prices, with the result that food prices will continue to spiral as petroleum becomes scarcer and more expensive.

The same companies that produce GM seeds also produce feedstocks for biofuels. This shows that these companies are not motivated by a desire to feed the world but by a desire to make a profit.

An additional cause of the 2007–2008 food crisis (apart from the rush to biofuels) was financial speculation in food commodity markets. This ongoing trend drives up prices for the crops that are traded internationally on a large scale, namely maize, wheat, and soy. One report on the topic concluded, "Food markets should serve the interests of people and not those of financial investors. . . . Given that hunger still exists in the world, even small price increases that are driven by financial investment are scandalous. We must not allow food to become a purely financial asset."

GM crops do not provide a solution to the problem of financial speculation in food markets.

Periodical and Internet Sources Bibliography

The following articles have been selected to supplement the diverse views presented in this chapter.

Sarah Berry	"Genetically Modified Health?," *Sydney Morning Herald*, April 27, 2012.
Biotechnology Industry Organization	"Food Crops Derived from Agricultural Biotechnology: Frequently Asked Questions About Food Labeling and Safety," March 2011.
Megan Clark	"GM Crops Can Play a Vital Role in Health and Food Security," *Sydney Morning Herald*, August 26, 2011.
Steve Connor	"If GM Crops Are Bad, Show Us the Evidence," *Independent* (UK), June 3, 2013.
Matthew Herper	"Green Genes: Are Genetically Modified Crops Eco-Friendly?," *Forbes*, February 11, 2010.
Institute for Responsible Technology	"State-of-the-Science on the Health Risks of GM Foods," February 15, 2010.
Amarnath K. Menon	"GM Food: How Safe Is It?," *India Today*, November 2, 2009.
Henry I. Miller	"Organic Is Overrated," *Defining Ideas*, July 26, 2012.
Henry I. Miller and Graham Brookes	"The GM Reactionaries," Project Syndicate, December 31, 2012.
Sue Neales	"An Inconvenient Truth," *Australian*, January 18, 2013.
Dinesh C. Sharma	"Toxin from GM Crops Found in Human Blood: Study," *India Today*, May 11, 2011.

CHAPTER 4

Regulations Regarding Genetically Modified Food

In the United States, the FDA Has Not Approved Any Genetically Modified Animals for Food

US Food and Drug Administration

In the following viewpoint, the US Food and Drug Administration (FDA) explains why it regulates genetically modified animals (GM) differently from GM plants. The FDA says that it has not approved any GM animals for food, but that GM animals are in development worldwide for food and other uses. The FDA is an agency of the US Department of Health and Human Services that is responsible for protecting public health by assuring the safety of human and veterinary drugs, biological products, medical devices, the food supply, cosmetics, and products that emit radiation.

As you read, consider the following questions:

1. According to the FDA, under what federal law are genetically engineered animals regulated?
2. What is a special concern regarding genetically engineered animals that the FDA says does not apply to genetically modified plants?
3. In what parts of the world outside of the United States are genetically enhanced fish being developed?

"Animal and Veterinary: Development & Approval Process, Genetic Engineering, General Q&A," US Food and Drug Administration, April 23, 2013.

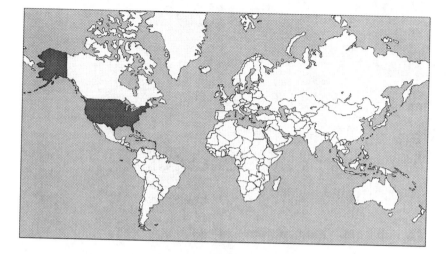

Many kinds of GE [genetically engineered] animals are in development. At this time, the largest class of GE animals is being developed for biopharm purposes—that is, they are intended to produce substances (for example, in their milk or blood) that can be used as human or animal pharmaceuticals. Another group of GE animals are under development for use as sources of scarce cells, tissues, or organs for transplantation into humans (xenotransplant sources). Yet others are intended for use as food and may be disease resistant, or have improved nutritional or growth characteristics. And others include animals that produce high-value industrial or consumer products, such as highly specific antimicrobials against human and animal pathogens (e.g., *E. coli* O157 or *Salmonella*).

The Benefits of GE Animals

How are GE animals different from conventional animals?

From a scientific perspective, the only intrinsic difference is that GE animals contain an rDNA construct that gives them a new trait or characteristic, such as producing a pharmaceutical or growing faster. The degree of difference between a GE animal and its conventional counterpart will depend on the new trait that the GE animal possesses. . . .

What are the known/potential benefits of genetically engineering animals?

The benefits depend entirely on the traits that are introduced. For example, scientists are attempting to develop GE cattle that are resistant to bovine spongiform encephalopathy, widely referred to as "mad cow disease." Some GE animals will grow more quickly, requiring less feed. Some GE animals have been altered to reduce their environmental impact by virtue of producing a lower level of pollutants in their wastes. Other GE animals may have improved fat composition, for example, increased levels of omega-3 fatty acids, providing a more healthful nutrient profile. Perhaps most importantly, scientists are developing GE animals that will produce certain human pharmaceuticals that are very difficult to produce in sufficient quantities by other means. An example of this is the potential ability to completely change the way in which certain chronic diseases, such as bleeding disorders, are treated. Currently, because clotting factors are so rare and difficult to obtain, people are treated only following acute attacks. If there were to be an increased supply of these clotting factors from GE animals, patients might be able to have much of their bleeding controlled by the regular administration of the medicine. In that way, these patients would potentially have a more normal ability to control bleeding. . . .

Many kinds of GE animals are in development.

The Regulation of GE Animals

How does the agency regulate GE animals and their products?

FDA regulates GE animals under the new animal drug provisions of the Federal Food, Drug, and Cosmetic Act (FFDCA), and FDA's regulations for new animal drugs. This guidance is intended to help industry understand the statutory and regulatory requirements as they apply to these animals, including those of the National Environmental Policy Act (NEPA), to inform the public about the process FDA is using to regulate GE animals, and to gather input from the public and the regulated industry. . . .

What are the elements of the new animal drug approval process?

The guidance recommends a review process that includes seven categories:

- *Product definition*: a broad statement characterizing the GE animal and the claim being made for the GE animal;

- *Molecular characterization of the construct*: a description of the rDNA construct and how it is assembled;

- *Molecular characterization of the GE animal lineage*: a description of the method by which the rDNA construct was introduced into the animal and whether it is stably maintained over time;

- *Phenotypic characterization of the GE animal*: comprehensive data on the characteristics of the GE animal and its health;

- *Durability plan*: the sponsor's plan to demonstrate that the modification will remain the same over time, and continue to have the same effect.

- *Environmental and food/feed safety*: the assessment of any environmental impacts, and for GE animals intended for food, that food from those GE animals is safe to eat for humans and/or animals;

- *Claim validation*: a demonstration that the GE animal does fulfill the product definition stated in the beginning of the review process. . . .

Why is the agency issuing a guidance and not a regulation?

Existing statutory requirements and FDA's existing regulations for new animal drugs are applicable to, and appropriate for, GE animals. Therefore, we do not believe we need a new law or regulation at this time to address GE animals and their products. However, we intend to issue additional guidance to describe the applicability of the new animal drug approval requirements to GE animals and their products.

The Animals Subject to Regulation

What is the legal basis on which GE animals are being regulated?

Under the Federal Food, Drug, and Cosmetic Act (FFDCA), "articles (other than food) intended to affect the structure or any function of the body of man or other animals" are defined as drugs. An rDNA construct that is in a GE animal and that is intended to affect the animal's structure or function meets the definition of a new animal drug. This is true regardless of whether the animals are intended for food or for some other purpose such as to produce pharmaceuticals. The FFDCA generally makes it unlawful to introduce unapproved new animal drugs into commerce. Therefore, pre-market approval requirements apply to GE animals before they are marketed, and potential significant environmental impacts, if any, must be examined before approval as required by the NEPA. The implementing regulations for new animal drugs are also applicable to rDNA constructs in GE animals.

Existing statutory requirements and FDA's existing regulations for new animal drugs are applicable to, and appropriate for, GE animals.

Does issuing a Guidance for Industry imply that this approach is voluntary?

No. A product that meets the definition of a new animal drug is generally required by statute and regulation to have an

FDA-approved New Animal Drug Application prior to marketing. In order for FDA to approve such an application, the FFDCA requires that the sponsor demonstrate that its product is safe and effective. Although the guidance does not itself impose any new requirements, we are issuing it to explain how existing statutory and regulatory requirements apply to GE animals and their products, and to provide recommendations on how sponsors may meet these responsibilities.

Are all GE animals subject to regulation under the new animal drug provisions of the act?

Yes, any animal containing an rDNA construct intended to alter its structure or function is subject to regulation by FDA prior to commercialization. However, based on risk, there are some GE animals for which the agency may not require an approval. In general, these include laboratory animals used for research. On a case-by-case basis, the agency may consider exercising enforcement discretion for GE animals of very low risk, such as it did for an aquarium fish genetically engineered to fluoresce in the dark. The agency does not anticipate exercising enforcement discretion for any GE animal of a species traditionally consumed as food and expects to require approval of all GE animals intended to go into the human food supply.

The Difference Between GE Animals and GE Plants

Why is this different from the way in which GE plants are being regulated?

There are a number of reasons for the difference. One overarching reason is that, unlike in some other countries, the US has not considered it appropriate to create a "novel food" regulation. That is, the US does not subject foods from GE organisms to a specific new regulation simply because of their GE status. Rather, the US has so far found that its existing laws can be applied to provide appropriate regulatory controls over GE foods. And because US law generally treats plants and animals differently, and treats food from plants differently from food from animals, the regulatory procedures for GE plants will, of necessity, differ from the regulatory procedures for GE animals.

The agency ... expects to require approval of all GE animals intended to go into the human food supply.

Another reason is that, unlike plants, animals can transmit diseases to humans, and in some very notable cases, are the origin of viral diseases in humans (e.g., swine flu). Depending on the nature of the modification to an animal, including the nature of any DNA sequences used to introduce or insert the rDNA construct into the animal, genetic engineering can enhance (or minimize) risks to human health. Although food from plants can be contaminated with human pathogens (usually from animals), and can thereby cause human illness, plants themselves ordinarily do not transmit human diseases. Genetic engineering does not change this. Therefore, GE animals can pose human health risks that would not arise with GE plants. The different regulatory approaches address these different risks.

Is the safety of food from GE animals being held to a different standard from the safety of food from GE plants?

Food sold in the United States must be safe, whether it is from plants or animals, and whether it is GE or non-GE. Although the regulatory process for food from GE animals is different than that for food from GE plants, as dictated by different statutory requirements, ultimately they both must be safe to be legally marketed. In fact, the food safety assessments are quite comparable, with some appropriate differences to accommodate the key differences between plants and animals, and look at the same information as recommended in the respective Codex [Alimentarius] guidelines that provide internationally accepted recommendations for assessing the safety of foods from GE plants and GE animals.

Are there special concerns related to GE animals that are not concerns for GE plants?

Most of the food safety issues are the same. However, all animals, including GE animals, can cause zoonotic diseases (animal diseases that cross over to humans) because some viruses and microorganisms from animals can infect humans. Because it is possible to genetically engineer animals using viruses or segments of DNA that can recombine and possibly transfer to humans or other animals and cause disease, there are some specific issues that must be evaluated in GE animals that are not relevant in GE plants. Addressing potential risks of introducing and spreading livestock pests or disease is also within the scope of USDA's APHIS [Animal and Plant Health Inspection Service] regulatory authority, as described in its RFI [request for information].

Are there GE animals in the food supply?

FDA has not approved any GE animals for food (or for any other purpose). During the pre-approval investigational phase, there are strong statutory and regulatory prohibitions against unreported movement of GE animals as well as against their disposal in the food supply unless explicitly approved by the FDA. In addition, there are strict requirements for good record-keeping during the investigational phase.

FDA has been working closely with developers of GE animals to ensure that they are aware of the regulations, particularly with respect to disposition of investigational animals. . . .

GE Animals Worldwide

Are GE animals or their products being developed in other countries? Have any been commercialized?

Yes, GE animals are being developed actively in many countries for both food and biopharmaceutical uses. For example, there have been multiple publications from Canadian developers of genetically engineered fish that grow more quickly, and pigs with smaller environmental footprints, as well as GE animals intended to produce human pharmaceuticals. In New Zealand, dairy researchers are looking to rDNA technology to affect the relative level of certain proteins in cows' milk to make it more suitable for cheese-making. China has a major agricultural program that employs rDNA technology to make more animal-based food available, and scientists from African countries are collaborating with aquaculturists in the US to develop GE tilapia that will grow quickly. Growth-enhanced fish are also being developed in Cuba. Scientists at the Roslin Institute in Scotland are developing GE chickens to produce pharmaceuticals in their eggs, as are other scientists in Korea. This is a very active area of research, and we expect that many products are likely to start reaching regulators, and then the market, within the next decade.

GE animals are being developed actively in many countries for both food and biopharmaceutical uses.

With respect to commercialization, many GE laboratory animals are in use in research laboratories around the world, including those GE laboratory animals that are sold to laboratories to perform various kinds of testing.

How do other countries regulate GE animals and their products?

Usually, when countries have pre-market approval requirements for GE foods or "novel foods," the requirements are the same whether the food comes from GE plants or GE animals. We anticipate that, like the US, most countries will evaluate the same information as that recommended in the Codex Alimentarius guideline on assessing the safety of foods from rDNA animals. We do not know what, if any, other requirements countries will put in place regarding GE animals.

What if a marketer wishes to import food into the US from a GE animal from another country?

FDA has a mechanism by which it can evaluate the safety of food from GE animals developed abroad and can establish an import tolerance to enable import of such food. In general, the information necessary to establish such import tolerance would be found in the sections of this guidance relevant to evaluating food safety and would be consistent with the information recommended for review in the Codex "Guideline for the Conduct of Food Safety Assessment of Foods Derived from Recombinant-DNA Animals." . . .

FDA will only approve food from GE animals that is safe to eat.

The Safety of GE Animals as Food

Will it be safe to eat the food from GE animals?

FDA will only approve food from GE animals that is safe to eat. FDA's food safety evaluation will look at the same information as that recommended internationally by Codex Alimentarius in its newly adopted guideline.

How will FDA evaluate the safety of meat or other food products from GE animals? How does the guidance compare with the recently approved Codex guideline for the food safety of foods from rDNA animals?

The FDA guidance essentially recommends the same information for evaluating food safety that the Codex guideline does: the characterization of the rDNA construct, the safety of the new substance produced as a result of the rDNA construct, the health status of the GE animals, and a demonstration that the composition of food produced from the GE animal is safe. . . .

Does the guidance have recommendations pertaining to mandatory tracking and labeling of GE animals?

The guidance does not have recommendations pertaining to mandatory tracking of GE animals. Developers of GE animals must, however, have labeling accompanying the animals. The guidance recommends that the labeling describe the GE animal (e.g., common name/breed/line, genus, species, GE animal line, rDNA construct), and its intended use. Where the labeling for a GE animal contains animal care or safety information (e.g., husbandry or containment), we recommend that the labeling accompany the animal throughout all stages of its life cycle.

Does the guidance have recommendations regarding the labeling of food from GE animals? Does such food have to be specially labeled?

The guidance doesn't explicitly address labeling of food from GE animals. FDA does not require that food from GE animals be labeled to indicate that it comes from GE animals, just as food from GE plants does not have to be labeled to indicate it comes from GE plants. However, if food from a GE animal is different from its non-engineered counterpart, for example, if it has a different nutritional profile, in general, that change would be material information that would have to be indicated in the labeling. Food marketers may voluntarily label their foods as coming from GE or non-GE animals, as long as the labeling is truthful and not misleading.

Don't Be Afraid of Genetic Modification

Emily Anthes

In the following viewpoint, Emily Anthes argues that resistance to US Food and Drug Administration (FDA) approval of genetically modified salmon is unwarranted. Anthes claims that the AquAdvantage salmon has many benefits and no risks, and that objection to its approval is political. She contends that the risks of continued delay on approval of genetically modified animals for food will damage innovation in the United States and will hinder the opportunity to address health and environmental problems. Anthes is author of Frankenstein's Cat: Cuddling Up to Biotech's Brave New Beasts.

As you read, consider the following questions:

1. According to the author, since what year has AquaBounty been waiting for the US Food and Drug Administration to approve its genetically modified salmon?

2. The author suggests that some members of Congress may oppose the AquAdvantage salmon for what reason?

3. Anthes claims that the political climate for genetically engineered animals is more favorable than the United States in what three countries?

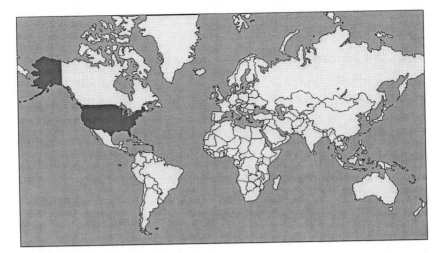

If patience is a virtue, then AquaBounty, a Massachusetts biotech company, might be the most virtuous entity on the planet.

In 1993, the company approached the Food and Drug Administration about selling a genetically modified salmon that grew faster than normal fish. In 1995, AquaBounty formally applied for approval. Last month, more than 17 years later, the public comment period, one of the last steps in the approval process, was finally supposed to conclude. But the FDA has extended the deadline—members of the public now have until late April to submit their thoughts on the AquAdvantage salmon. It's just one more delay in a process that's dragged on far too long.

The AquAdvantage fish is an Atlantic salmon that carries two foreign bits of DNA: a growth hormone gene from the chinook salmon that is under the control of a genetic "switch" from the ocean pout, an eel-like fish that lives in the chilly deep. Normally, Atlantic salmon produce growth hormone only in the warm summer months, but these genetic adjustments let the fish churn it out year-round. As a result, the AquAdvantage salmon typically reach their adult size in a year and a half, rather than three years.

If the modified fish is approved, which could still happen later this year, it will be the first transgenic animal to officially enter the human food supply. Appropriately, it has been subjected to rigorous reviews, with scientists all over the country weighing in on whether it is fit for human consumption and what might happen if it was to make its way into the wild. Some environmentalists fear that the modified salmon might wriggle free from fish farms, start reproducing, and ultimately drive wild salmon populations to extinction.

But scientists, including the FDA's experts, have concluded that the fish is just as safe to eat as conventional salmon and that, raised in isolated tanks, it poses little risk to wild populations.

This decision isn't meant to be made quickly; due scientific diligence requires time. But some suspect that political considerations have played a role in drawing the approval process out to tortuous lengths. Many of the members of Congress who oppose the modified fish represent states with strong salmon industries. And some nonprofit groups seem to be opposing the modified salmon reflexively, as part of an agenda to oppose all animal biotechnology, regardless of its safety or potential benefits.

Even the White House might be playing politics with the salmon. One step in the approval process is the preparation of an environmental assessment on the fish's potential risks. In May of last year, the FDA commissioner said that a draft would be released "very soon." Months passed.

Scientists, including the FDA's experts, have concluded that the fish is just as safe to eat as conventional salmon.

In December, Jon Entine, the executive director of the Genetic Literacy Project, a nonpartisan, nonprofit group that promotes education about biotechnology issues, wrote an article in *Slate* suggesting that the holdup wasn't with the FDA, which had completed the report, but with the Obama administration, which had just finished a re-election campaign. He wrote, "The delay, sources within the government say, came after meetings with the White House, which was debating the political implications of approving the GM salmon, a move likely to infuriate a portion of its base." A few days after the article appeared, the FDA published its assessment. The date on the report—May 4, 2012—seemed to confirm Mr. Entine's account that it had been ready for months.

The publication of that assessment initiated the public comment period, now extended to April. After reviewing the comments—more than 30,000, so far—the FDA will be free to issue its final ruling.

We should all be rooting for the agency to do the right thing and approve the AquAdvantage salmon. It's a healthy and relatively cheap food source that, as global demand for fish increases, can take some pressure off our wild fish stocks. But most important, a rejection will have a chilling effect on biotechnological innovation in this country.

Some scientists may move abroad, to China, Argentina, India or another nation where the political climate is more favorable. (Indeed, some have already done so—researchers at the University of California, Davis, who have developed goats whose modified milk could be used to treat and prevent childhood diarrhea, are moving much of their operation to Brazil.) Others may decide not to pursue such research at all. If a company that has done everything right can't get its product approved, who else will be foolish enough to embark upon this kind of research? Who will finance it?

Of course, all this would be just fine with some antibiotech groups, which traffic in scare tactics rather than science. But it shouldn't be fine with the rest of us.

Genetically engineered animals could do real good for the world. Scientists at Cambridge University and Scotland's Roslin Institute—the facility that created Dolly, the cloned sheep,

Genetically Altered Fish?

The Food and Drug Administration will decide whether Atlantic salmon genetically engineered to grow faster than their natural relatives can be allowed to be raised and sold as food in the United States.

Bred to grow faster   Altered fish can reach adult size in 16–28 months instead of 36 months for normal Atlantic salmon.

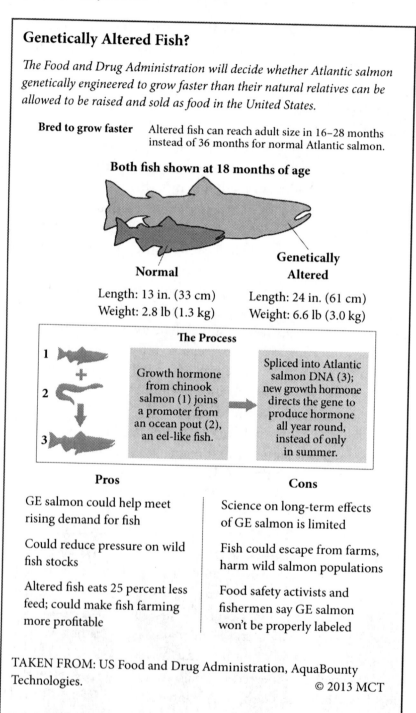

Both fish shown at 18 months of age

Normal
Length: 13 in. (33 cm)
Weight: 2.8 lb (1.3 kg)

Genetically Altered
Length: 24 in. (61 cm)
Weight: 6.6 lb (3.0 kg)

The Process

1
2
3

Growth hormone from chinook salmon (1) joins a promoter from an ocean pout (2), an eel-like fish.

Spliced into Atlantic salmon DNA (3); new growth hormone directs the gene to produce hormone all year round, instead of only in summer.

Pros

GE salmon could help meet rising demand for fish

Could reduce pressure on wild fish stocks

Altered fish eats 25 percent less feed; could make fish farming more profitable

Cons

Science on long-term effects of GE salmon is limited

Fish could escape from farms, harm wild salmon populations

Food safety activists and fishermen say GE salmon won't be properly labeled

TAKEN FROM: US Food and Drug Administration, AquaBounty Technologies.

© 2013 MCT

in 1996—have been working to genetically engineer chickens that are resistant to bird flu. They haven't pulled that feat off yet, but they have managed to engineer birds that can't spread the flu to others in their flock, which is a good start. Given how hard it is to develop vaccines to combat the rapidly evolving flu virus, this genetic modification could end up saving the lives of many birds, and perhaps humans.

Then there's the Enviropig, a swine that has been genetically modified to excrete less phosphorus. Phosphorus in animal waste is a major cause of water pollution, and as the world's appetite for meat increases, it's becoming a more urgent problem. The first Enviropig, created by scientists at the University of Guelph, in Canada, was born in 1999, and researchers applied to both the FDA and Health Canada for permission to sell the pigs as food.

But last spring, while the applications were still pending, the scientists lost their funding from Ontario Pork, an association of Canadian hog farmers, and couldn't find another industry partner. (It's hard to blame investors for their reluctance, given the public sentiment in Canada and the United States, as well as the uncertain regulatory landscape.) The pigs were euthanized in May.

Genetically engineered animals could do real good for the world.

The FDA must make sure that other promising genetically modified animals don't come to the same end. Of course every application needs to be painstakingly evaluated, and not every modified animal should be approved. But in cases like AquaBounty's, where all the available evidence indicates that the animals are safe, we shouldn't let political calculations or unfounded fears keep these products off the market. If we do that, we'll be closing the door on innovations that could help us face the public health and environmental threats of the future, saving countless animals—and perhaps ourselves.

In the United Kingdom, Regulations Are Hampering Genetic Modification Technology

Owen Paterson

In the following viewpoint, Owen Paterson argues that the resistance to allowing genetically modified (GM) crops in Great Britain and the rest of the European Union is not related to the facts about the technology. Paterson claims that GM crops have environmental, economic, and health benefits, and there is no safety reason to continue the stringent restrictions on their cultivation, especially given that GM livestock feed is imported from elsewhere. Paterson is a member of Parliament for the United Kingdom and secretary of state for environment, food, and rural affairs.

As you read, consider the following questions:

1. According to the author, since 1996, by what factor has the global use of genetically modified crops increased?

2. What percentage of farmers who grew genetically modified crops in 2012 were small, resource-poor farmers in developing countries, according to Paterson?

3. According to the author, how many genetically modified crops have been approved for cultivation in the European Union in the last fourteen years?

Owen Paterson, "Rt Hon Owen Paterson MP Speech to Rothamsted Research," UK Department for Environment, Food & Rural Affairs, June 20, 2012.

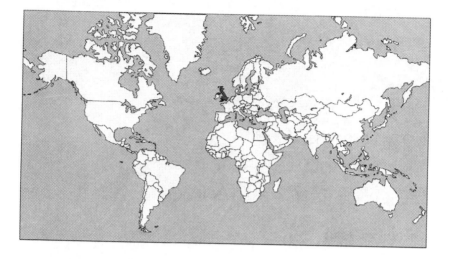

The recent OECD-FAO [Organisation for Economic Co-operation and Development–United Nations Food and Agriculture Organization] agricultural outlook for 2012 to 2021 concluded that agricultural production needs to increase by 60 per cent over the next 40 years to meet the rising demand for food. Our growing population will put further pressures on land, energy and water—creating a food security risk. We need to adopt new technologies, of which GM [genetic modification] is one, if we are to combat this.

The Promise of New Technology

[American agronomist Norman] Borlaug and others harnessed innovation to completely change the way we farm. For example, it has been estimated that the production of a given quantity of a crop now requires 65 per cent less land than it did in 1961. Between 1967 and 2007 world food production increased by 115 per cent but land use only increased by eight per cent. Indur Goklany has calculated that if we tried to support today's population using the production methods of the 1950s, instead of farming 38 per cent of all land, we would need to use 82 per cent.

The political debate here in Britain in recent decades has been based on a false premise: that we can either produce more or look after the environment. The truth is we need to do both and we won't be able to do so unless we embrace innovation in all areas—agriculture, agronomy, commerce and technology.

We have been adapting genetics through plant breeding for centuries. Recent advances such as the sequencing of the wheat genome by UK [United Kingdom] scientists and the development of "superwheat" over at NIAB [National Institute of Agricultural Botany] in Cambridge show what can be done with conventional cross-breeding. But we'll need to use all available tools if we are to address the serious challenges we face.

Used properly, the advanced plant-breeding technique of GM promises effective ways to protect or increase crop yields. It can also combat the damaging effects of unpredictable weather and disease on crops. It has the potential to reduce fertiliser and chemical use, improve the efficiency of agricultural production and reduce post-harvest losses.

Even more excitingly, if we use cultivated land more efficiently, we could free up space for biodiversity, nature and wilderness, something I know a number of commentators have been calling for. Research undertaken by a team at Rockefeller University has found that over the course of the next 50 years new technology, combined with improved agricultural practices across the world, could release an area 2.5 times the size of France from cultivation.

The Global Position of the United Kingdom

Since 1996 there has been a 100-fold increase in the global use of GM. Last year [2011], GM crops were grown by 17.3 million farmers in 28 countries on 170 million hectares. That's 12 per cent of all arable land—an area around 7 times the size of the United Kingdom.

Farmers wouldn't grow these crops if they didn't benefit from doing so.

Governments wouldn't licence these technologies if they didn't recognise the economic, environmental and public benefits.

Consumers wouldn't buy these products if they didn't think they were safe and cost-effective.

At the moment Europe is missing out. Less than 0.1% of global GM cultivation occurred in the EU [European Union]. While the rest of the world is ploughing ahead and reaping the benefits of new technologies, Europe risks being left behind. We cannot afford to let that happen. The use of GM could be as transformative as the original agricultural revolution. The UK should be at the forefront of that, now, as it was then.

I want the UK to have a leading role in feeding the world and increasing the resilience of global food supplies, not standing by watching others take the lead and forge ahead. The UK is the natural home for science research. I want companies and research providers to know that the UK is the best place for them to carry out their work. If there are barriers preventing them from undertaking their activities here, this government will help overcome them.

While the rest of the world is ploughing ahead and reaping the benefits of new technologies, Europe risks being left behind.

The Economic Benefits of GM Crops

The current range of GM crops was designed to offer farmers easier, quicker and cheaper control over pests or weeds. Evidence demonstrates that they have delivered on this, providing economic benefits for farmers and consumers alike.

Europe benefits hugely from the GM crops grown in the rest of the world.

The EU is the world's biggest net importer of agricultural goods and we rely on shipments of key commodities to support our livestock system. According to the European Feed Manufacturers' Association, about 85 per cent of the EU's compound livestock feed production is now labelled to indicate that it contains GM or GM-derived material.

In April, four of our major supermarket chains announced that they could no longer guarantee that no GM feed would be used in the production of their own-brand eggs and poultry due to the difficulty and expense of securing non-GM feed. This was a necessary step and the supermarkets were right to make it absolutely clear that the use of such products in no way constitutes a food safety issue. Such transparency is vital to ensure that consumers are able to make an informed choice.

At the beginning of the year I met the Brazilian agriculture minister in Berlin. He told me that GM soya is 30 per cent more cost-effective than conventional soya. Soya is a key protein source for our livestock. It's an integral part of the global food system.

About 85 per cent of the EU's compound livestock feed production is now labelled to indicate that it contains GM or GM-derived material.

Farmers worldwide grow GM soya because it makes business sense for them to do so. The adoption rates for GM soya stand at 88 per cent in Brazil, 93 per cent in the US and 100 per cent in Argentina.

Europe imports GM soya from those countries because it makes economic sense for us to do so. Sourcing non-GM soya can now cost between an extra £100–150 per tonne. Without imports of GM crops our food and particularly meat products would be more expensive. . . .

Pest and Disease Resistance

GM has already been used to make crops that can resist attack from specific insect pests or plant diseases. Other traits are being developed, including using scientific expertise here in the UK.

The fungal disease late blight remains a significant problem for potato growers. Tackling blight can require up to 15 separate fungicide applications a year. Before we skim over that fact, in practical terms that might see a heavy sprayer criss-crossing a field, burning diesel, compacting the soil, spraying the crop including surrounding plants and insects and emitting fumes. All this, up to 15 times a year.

The total annual cost to the UK of controlling this disease is around £60 million and even then crops can still be affected. Both the Sainsbury Laboratory and [chemical company] BASF have trialled different types of GM blight-resistant potato in the UK. If this type of crop can be successfully deployed, it could deliver both economic and environmental benefits. As well as protection against devastating plant diseases, inputs like pesticides and fuel could be dramatically reduced.

I'm dismayed by BASF's recent decision to withdraw their blight-resistant potato from the EU approvals system. I don't blame BASF. They simply took a commercial decision in response to current market and regulatory conditions. But the fact that those conditions have deteriorated to the point where a potentially economically beneficial and environmentally friendly crop has no prospect of gaining market access should be a wake-up call.

The Environmental Benefits of Biotechnology

Thanks to biotechnology, farmers around the world have been able to protect yields, prevent damage from insects and pests and reduce farming's impact on the environment. There is also evidence which points to GM crops delivering further environmental benefits such as reduced soil erosion and reduced use of fuel and chemicals.

We are currently debating the effects of pesticides on bees and other insects. In other parts of the world where GM crops are grown, plants are better protected against pests and insects are better protected against accidentally being sprayed. I recently spoke to a farmer in North Carolina who has been able to do away with all of his spraying equipment as a result of GM technology.

The farmer benefits. The consumer benefits. The environment benefits.

The farmer benefits. The consumer benefits. The environment benefits.

The Development of Efficient Nitrogen Use

Enabling crops to use nitrogen more efficiently would mean less artificial fertiliser and reduced fuel use. Such traits are currently being developed commercially and field trials of nitrogen-efficient GM wheat and barley are scheduled to take place in Australia between 2013 and 2015.

In the longer term, research is under way into developing cereal crops that can 'fix' their own nitrogen. This could largely remove the need for farmers to apply chemical fertilisers. The environmental benefits of these kinds of crops are huge. Less spraying. Fewer chemicals going onto crops and the surrounding area. Fewer applications requiring less fuel. Less runoff into our sensitive and vitally important water courses.

173

The challenge here is enormous, as are the potential benefits. This is why I welcome the £6.4 million grant provided by the Gates Foundation last year to the John Innes Centre at Norwich to research this. This type of large-scale investment into a global problem using UK scientific expertise is something we should be proud of. I hope other research providers will look to the UK first when making their investment decisions.

The International Benefits of Genetic Modification

The benefits of GM do not just extend to developed countries.

It's estimated that around 90 per cent of those farmers who grew GM crops in 2012 were small, resource-poor farmers in developing countries. Over 7 million farmers in China and a further 7 million farmers in India decided to grow insect-resistant GM cotton because of the significant benefits.

A GM drought-tolerant maize is now being grown in the USA and is undergoing field trials in Kenya, South Africa and Uganda. The Australians are currently researching GM drought-tolerant wheat. The potential for such crops to make a real difference to some of the world's poorest countries is tremendous.

As well as drought tolerance, scientists are also exploring the possible development of other GM crops which are flood tolerant, salt tolerant or resistant to extreme temperature fluctuations. All of these promise to allow agricultural production on land previously considered marginal.

In Uganda, field trials of disease-resistant and nutritionally enhanced GM bananas are at an advanced stage. Nigerian scientists have responded to the devastating economic impact of the "mung moth" on the black-eyed pea harvest by developing a pest-resistant variety. Nigerian farmers currently lose nearly £200 million worth of crops to the parasite each year and spend a further £300 million importing pesticides to deal with it.

The Health and Nutritional Benefits

There are also GM crops in the pipeline promising health and nutritional benefits, the impact of which could be most acutely felt in the developing world. GM crops with enhanced omega-3 properties are now close to market. Nigeria is undertaking field trials of GM bio-fortified cassava and sorghum with enhanced vitamin A and iron content.

Golden Rice was first created in 1999 by German professors [Ingo] Potrykus and [Peter] Beyer and a not-for-profit independent research institute to help tackle vitamin A deficiency. It is the leading cause of irreversible blindness in children. The World Health Organization estimates that this results in up to 500,000 children going blind a year—250,000 of whom will lose their lives within a year. The problem is particularly severe in Southeast Asia.

Golden Rice was only possible as a result of genetic engineering. We should all reflect on the fact that it is 15 years since it was developed and attempts to deploy it have been thwarted. This is despite the seeds being offered for free to those who need them most. In that time, more than seven million children [have] gone blind or died.

Biotechnology can also help develop plant-made pharmaceuticals which produce proteins that can be used, for example, in influenza vaccines or for insulin production.

GM offers real opportunities to develop crops that provide better resilience to extremes of weather and land conditions. There is the potential to add extra nutrients that can directly help people in developing countries who are vulnerable to nutrient deficiencies in their diets. As the world's population continues to increase, access to these technologies becomes even more important.

The Safety of GM Crops

As with all technologies, public and environmental safety is paramount. The reality is that in Europe and elsewhere, GM is perhaps the most regulated of all agricultural technologies.

There are some that describe GM crops as "Frankenfoods", deliberately termed to imply that they pose a risk to human health and the environment.

The truth is that products are subject to extensive testing and development in tightly controlled conditions—progressing from laboratory, to glasshouse, to field trials only when it's safe to do so.

After all of the pre-commercial testing, marketing applications for GM products must undergo a comprehensive case-by-case scientific risk assessment. This is undertaken by independent scientists in the European Food Safety Authority. In the UK, we also receive independent advice from committees of world-leading scientific experts.

The reality is that in Europe and elsewhere, GM is perhaps the most regulated of all agricultural technologies.

Over the past 25 years the EU alone has funded more than 50 projects on GM safety involving more than 400 independent research groups at a cost of around £260 million. Summary reports produced by the European Commission in 2000 and in 2010 reached two powerful conclusions.

First, there was no scientific evidence associating GMOs [genetically modified organisms] with higher risks for the environment or for food and feed safety than conventional plants and organisms.

Second, the use of more precise technology and the greater regulatory scrutiny probably makes GMOs even safer than conventional plants and food.

The European Commission's chief scientist Professor Anne Glover has recently said that "there is no substantiated case of any adverse impact on human health, animal health or environmental health".

The Impact on Agriculture

Weed resistance is also often highlighted as an environmental problem associated with GM crops but it's something that occurs in conventional cropping too. It's not a GM issue; it's a crop management issue. Farmers of both types of crops can take steps to mitigate against this, through effective management of rotations.

Concerns have also been voiced about the ability for GM crops to coexist alongside conventional and organic agriculture. I would like to assure the public that this is an issue that we take seriously. As and when GM crops come through which could be grown here, we will introduce measures to segregate them from conventional and organic crops so that all economic interests are protected.

Agriculture is a highly segregated sector. Even though we don't currently grow any GM crops commercially, our industry is already able to protect the integrity of crops intended for different market outlets. They do this, for example, to maintain the vigour of conventional hybrid seeds. We also have the experience of other countries who are growing GM crops and the European [Coexistence] Bureau, which issues best practice guidelines for the effective management of GM crops.

With regard to consumer choice, I would like to make clear that no one, least of all me, is suggesting the wholesale adoption of GM in the UK's food chain. I believe that people should be able to walk into a supermarket and choose whether to buy local organic potatoes or those produced from a blight-resistant GM variety grown in the UK. Whatever the product, whatever its origin, people should be confident in the knowledge that it is safe to eat and grown sustainably. Our policy should be based on sound science and strong safeguards.

No one wants to see a biotech monoculture in UK farming. Diversity and choice are a force for good.

The Current EU Situation

I am convinced that the EU has the most robust and comprehensive safety system for GMOs in the world. Not only do we have access to independent scientists in the European Food Safety Authority but there are scientific and regulatory authorities in each of the member states who will assess GM crops and products before they are approved for use.

As I have already outlined, the EU is already a mass consumer of GM crops—primarily through imports of livestock feed. More than 40 GM products have received the necessary approval for food and feed use in the EU without any health or environmental issues arising.

Despite this, the picture is very different when it comes to the approval of GM crops which are destined to be grown within the EU. Only 1 crop has been approved for cultivation in the last 14 years. GM products which have passed the safety assessments remain stuck in the pipeline. I sympathise with the European Commissioner who has to grapple with divergent views across the EU.

I want British researchers and farmers to be able to develop the latest technologies so that they can reap the economic and environmental benefits.

While I acknowledge the views of other member states, I want British researchers and farmers to be able to develop the latest technologies so that they can reap the economic and environmental benefits. At the moment we are expecting them to respond to the challenges of global food security with one hand tied behind their back.

This is deeply regrettable.

It means that the prospect of crops coming through which offer solutions to UK-specific problems are many years away.

The Need for Market Access

We risk driving scientific and intellectual capital away from Europe for good. This will reduce our ability to develop and deploy crucial tools which could help ensure European agricultural production meets future demands while protecting the environment.

We need evidence-based regulation and decision making in the EU. Consumers need accurate information in order to make informed choices. The market should then decide if a GM product is viable.

Farmers are also consumers but right now that market is not functioning and they are being denied choice.

That's why I want to explore ways of getting the EU system working, as this will encourage further investment and innovation.

I'm not in any way suggesting that EU safeguards should be watered down. They are vital. But we must find a way to allow fair market access for products which have undergone a rigorous case-by-case safety assessment.

The Impact of the EU's Position on the Developing World

In April 2012, ministers from 24 African states signed a joint communiqué which endorsed the use of biotechnology as one means of enhancing agricultural productivity in Africa.

Yet there is evidence that the EU's treatment of GM is having a detrimental impact on developing countries. Europe's attitude to GM is interpreted as a sign that the technology is dangerous. And this can generate unwarranted resistance to the technology in the parts of the world that most need access to agricultural innovations. Developing countries also fear being locked out of EU markets if they use a GM crop that is unapproved in the EU. Only recently, Professor Calestous Juma argued that the current situation "was to the great detriment of Africa" and that "opposition to new technologies may cast a dark shadow over the prospects of feeding the world."

We have a responsibility in the EU to ensure that we set the right framework to enable developing countries to take their own informed decisions about whether GM solutions are appropriate for them.

In Nigeria, Reluctance to Allow Genetically Modified Crops Should Not Be Ignored

Friends of the Earth International

In the following viewpoint, Friends of the Earth International argues that legislation is being pushed through in Nigeria to allow genetically modified (GM) crops, despite the fact that there is widespread grassroots opposition. The author claims that the initiatives in favor of GM crops were pushed by corporate-backed international nongovernmental organizations, ignoring the past failures of GM crops and the non-GM alternatives. Friends of the Earth International is a network of environmental organizations in more than seventy countries.

As you read, consider the following questions:

1. What did the Gates Foundation do in August 2010 that, according to the author, angered farmers, social movements, and civil society groups?

2. The Donald Danforth Plant Science Center in Nigeria was given a grant by the Gates Foundation to do what?

3. How does the World Health Organization suggest that vitamin A deficiency be tackled, according to Friends of the Earth International?

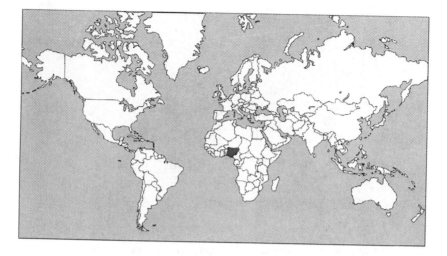

Africa has seen a major increase in food production in recent decades but 265 million sub-Saharan Africans still go
hungry. This food crisis is being used to justify opening up
Africa as the new test bed for GMOs [genetically modified or-
ganisms]: GM technology proponents argue that the technology can combat hunger, poverty and climate change. Yet, many
Africans continue to eschew expensive, dangerous GM crop
cultivation that can increase indebtedness and does nothing to
withstand erratic weather conditions, as Friends of the Earth
International has documented.

This reluctance is being met by corporate-backed, pro-GM
initiatives promoted by the Gates Foundation and Alliance for
a Green Revolution in Africa (AGRA). This poses grave threats
to traditional, sustainable farming practices that could feed
the continent and significantly reduce levels of poverty.

The Gates Foundation Buys into Monsanto

The Bill & Melinda Gates Foundation, founded in 1994, exerts
a major influence on global agricultural policy. It manages total grants of US$24 billion, which finance the foundation's
projects. The Gates Foundation claims to promote "new techniques to help farmers in developing countries grow more

food and earn more money" whilst openly supporting genetic engineering projects in Africa and other developing countries. Nearly 80% of Gates Foundation funding in Kenya involves biotechnology and there have been over $100 million in grants to organisations connected to Monsanto.

The revolving door between the foundation and Monsanto was flung wide open when the foundation bought US$23 million worth of Monsanto shares, in August 2010. Farmers, social movements and civil society organisations reacted with outrage. La Via Campesina, the global peasant movement, has condemned this acquisition of Monsanto shares. Chavannes Jean-Baptiste of the Haitian Peasant Movement of Papaye and Caribbean coordinator of La Via Campesina stated:

> "It is really shocking for the peasant organizations and social movements in Haiti to learn about the decision of the Bill & Melinda Gates Foundation to buy Monsanto shares while it is giving money for agricultural projects in Haiti that promote the company's seed and agrochemicals."

AGRA's Unwelcome Green Revolution

Along with the Rockefeller Foundation, the Gates Foundation is supporting the implementation of the controversial Alliance for a Green Revolution in Africa (AGRA) to the tune of US$265 million. AGRA consists of a team of scientists, economists and business leaders, including from the biotech industry, and [former secretary-general of the United Nations] Kofi Annan is the chair of its board.

AGRA is prising open the African continent to GM seeds and pesticides sold by corporations such as Monsanto, DuPont and Syngenta. In contrast to the approach by the Gates Foundation and AGRA, a major study by UNCTAD [United Nations Conference on Trade and Development] and UNEP [United Nations Environment Programme] that examined organic agricultural practices throughout Africa concluded these could reduce poverty, increase yields and incomes whilst protecting the environment.

African farmers and environmentalists have challenged the Gates Foundation and AGRA's initiatives that disregard the structural causes of hunger and poverty, and instead promote policies that undermine traditional knowledge and farming systems.

West African farmers [of the International Institute for Environment and Development] have clearly rejected such corporate-driven initiatives by demanding "a fundamental re-orientation of public research away from a focus on input-intensive farming and the development of new GM seeds, to instead support agriculture which does not require high chemical inputs, to improve local seeds and landraces, and to regenerate local food systems and markets".

The Nigerian Government

Nigeria, Africa's most populous country with 150 million citizens, is on the biotech industry's radar. For example, the Gates Foundation has granted the Donald Danforth Plant Science Center US$5.4 million to conduct trials for genetically modified banana, rice, sorghum and cassava plants that contain increased amounts of vitamins, minerals and proteins.

African farmers and environmentalists have challenged the Gates Foundation and AGRA's initiatives that disregard the structural causes of hunger and poverty.

Millions of Nigerians depend on cassava as a staple food crop. On behalf of the Danforth Center and biotech corporations, the Nigerian National Root Crops Research Institute (NRCRI) has been conducting "contained" field trials of genetically modified 'Super Cassava' on a plot on the banks of Qua Iboe River, Abia State.

The Monsanto Corporation

Monsanto—the leading source of genetically modified (GM) crops—has its headquarters in Missouri, USA, and over 400 facilities in 66 countries. It generated net sales that amounted to more than US$11.8 billion in 2011.

The Monsanto enterprise was originally founded in 1901 as a company manufacturing chemicals. As it grew, Monsanto started producing sweeteners for food companies, agricultural chemicals including DDT, toxic PCBs for industries, components of Agent Orange for the military, and bovine growth hormone.

In the 1980s and 1990s, Monsanto reinvented itself by focusing on genetic modification processes. This shift was consolidated as GM crops became commercialised in the mid-1990s, and the global sale of seeds became dominated by Monsanto as it bought up major seed companies. By 2005, Monsanto was the world's largest seed company, providing the technology for 90% of GM crops around the world. Monsanto controls 27% of the commercial seed market. It controls 90% of the seed market for soy. However, the application of the genetic modification process has been confined to a limited number of commercial crops such as soy, maize and cotton.

Monsanto's control over seed varieties has been bolstered by its aggressive implementation of patent rights: It frequently compels farmers who purchase its patented seeds to sign agreements that ban them from saving seeds and replanting them. Farmers breaking this agreement can face legal action.

La Via Campesina, Friends of the Earth International, and Combat Monsanto, "Combatting Monsanto: Grassroots Resistance to the Corporate Power of Agribusiness in the Era of the 'Green Economy' and a Changing Climate," March 2012.

The Danforth Center claims that the cassava-based diet of over 250 million sub-Saharan Africans does not provide complete nutrition. Their solution is to develop nutritious, higher-yielding cassava with traits to deliver enhanced levels of zinc, iron, protein, vitamin A, vitamin E, improved post-harvest durability, and improved resistance against viral diseases. Yet efforts to engineer the cassava to resist cassava leaf mosaic disease have failed. Nigerian ministry of agriculture officials have confirmed that there are over 40 conventionally bred hybrid varieties of cassava that already have the capacity to resist this disease.

The Lessons from GM Golden Rice

Nutrient-enhanced GM crops were once hailed as a panacea for vitamin A deficiency, when the infamous Golden Rice, which was lauded as being able to save one million children a year, made it to the front page of *Time* magazine in 2000.

Despite many African countries being unreceptive and sceptical of GM, new pro-GM legislation is being pushed through in Nigeria.

Yet trials failed to develop high levels of vitamin A and scientists have expressed major disquiet over potential negative health impacts. In February 2009, a group of international scientists and experts expressed outrage over health threats from GM Golden Rice clinical trials being conducted on adults and children at Tufts University in Massachusetts, as there has never been a regulatory approval process on its effects anywhere in the world.

Recent analysis highlights that after almost two decades of research and development, GM 'golden' rice has not made any impact on the prevalence of vitamin A deficiency. This has drawn attention and resources, which could otherwise have been targeted at supporting sustainable, agroecological farming.

While it is true that diets based only on rice and cassava are not sufficient for nutrition, there are simple solutions to ensure a healthy intake of vitamins and minerals. The World Health Organization (WHO) recommends tackling vitamin A deficiency through the promotion of breast-feeding and development of gardening practices. WHO malnutrition expert Francesco Branca suggests that providing supplements, fortifying existing foods with vitamin A, and teaching people to grow carrots or certain leafy vegetables are more promising approaches than relying on the unsubstantiated technology of Golden Rice.

The Push for Pro-GM Policies

Despite many African countries being unreceptive and sceptical of GM, new pro-GM legislation is being pushed through in Nigeria. In December 2009, public health and environmental concerns were marginalised as a draft bill was progressing through Parliament to pave the way for the introduction of GMOs. As the bill was passed the chairman of the House Committee on Agriculture, Hon. Gbenga Makanjuola, stated that biotechnology was a technology that could not be stopped and must be accepted by Nigerians.

During the discussions on the bill, while pro-GM commercial farmers, scientists, professors and biotech NGOs from across the nation had ample time to make their points, critical opponents such as Friends of the Earth Nigeria/ERA [Environmental Rights Action], consumer groups, women and youth groups and other organisations were either not allowed to voice their concerns or had to rush them in a fraction of the time allocated to the GM proponents. According to provisions of the draft bill, yet to be passed through the Senate, it appears that GMOs may be approved without taking into account public opinion or opposition.

Friends of the Earth Nigeria/ERA is currently challenging the National Biotechnology Development Agency (NABDA) of

Nigeria for attempting to pass this bill without greater partici-
pation of all stakeholders, including farmers, and is initiating
a public debate to consider health and environmental implications.

Periodical and Internet Sources Bibliography

The following articles have been selected to supplement the diverse views presented in this chapter.

William Y. Brown	"It's Time for a New Biotechnology Law," Brookings Institution, July 27, 2011.
Christian Science Monitor	"Frankenfish—Genetically Modified Salmon—Take Food and Ecology to a New Level," September 22, 2010.
Nina V. Fedoroff	"Engineering Food for All," *New York Times*, August 18, 2011.
Hans Herren and Marcia Ishii-Eiteman	"Genetically Modified Crops Are Not the Answer," *The Hill*, April 22, 2010.
Gregory Jaffe	"Regulatory Procedure Necessary for GE Food," *The Hill*, October 1, 2010.
Marcel Kuntz, John Davison, and Agnès E. Ricroch	"GMO Ban: Risks for Science-Based Assessments," EurActiv.com, March 7, 2012.
Henry Miller	"The FDA Needs Egging On," *Guardian* (UK), August 24, 2010.
Chuck Norris	"The US, the UN and Genetic Engineering," *Human Events*, September 27, 2011.
Greg Odogwu	"Is Nigeria Ready for Genetically Modified Foods?," *Punch*, August 1, 2013.
Tom Philpott	"Wait, Did the USDA Just Deregulate All New Genetically Modified Crops?," *Mother Jones*, July 8, 2011.
Washington Post	"Labels May Not Be Necessary on Genetically Altered Foods," September 23, 2010.

For Further Discussion

Chapter 1

1. Drawing on the viewpoints of this chapter, suggest at least three reasons why attitudes toward genetically modified food vary so widely around the world.

Chapter 2

1. Food & Water Watch claims that genetically modified crops harm farmers by contamination and suggests that farmers be allowed to recover damages when this happens. Do you think Roger Beachy would agree with this? Why or why not?

2. Per Pinstrup-Andersen contends that arguments against genetically modified crops fail, whereas Peter Melchett claims that they are based on science. Pick at least one argument where they disagree, explain both sides, and suggest a justification for choosing one side.

Chapter 3

1. Ramez Naam says that several reputable scientific bodies worldwide have concluded that genetically modified food is safe. Would this evidence convince Ari LeVaux? Drawing upon the text of both viewpoints, defend your answer.

2. Neil Perry and Martin Boetz argue that non-transgenic food has been "tested" for thousands of years. Are they suggesting that genetically modified food be tested for thousands of years before being allowed? Would this be a reasonable request?

Chapter 4

1. Based on the viewpoints in this volume, which author in this chapter do you think makes the most compelling case for a particular regulation, or lack thereof? Explain your answer drawing upon at least three authors' viewpoints.

Organizations to Contact

The editors have compiled the following list of organizations concerned with the issues debated in this book. The descriptions are derived from materials provided by the organizations. All have publications or information available for interested readers. The list was compiled on the date of publication of the present volume; the information provided here may change. Be aware that many organizations take several weeks or longer to respond to inquiries, so allow as much time as possible.

Biotechnology Industry Organization (BIO)

1201 Maryland Avenue SW, Suite 900, Washington, DC 20024
(202) 962-9200 • fax: (202) 488-6301
e-mail: info@bio.org
website: www.bio.org

The Biotechnology Industry Organization (BIO) represents biotechnology companies, academic institutions, state biotechnology centers, and related organizations that support the use of biotechnology. BIO advocates for its corporate members by championing the use of biotechnology. BIO publishes advocacy on issues related to genetic engineering, including "Feeding the World: How to Feed Seven Billion People."

Center for Food Safety (CFS)

660 Pennsylvania Avenue SE, #302, Washington, DC 20003
(202) 547-9359 • fax: (202) 547-9429
e-mail: office@centerforfoodsafety.org
website: www.centerforfoodsafety.org

The Center for Food Safety (CFS) is a nonprofit public interest organization established for the purpose of challenging harmful food production technologies and promoting sustainable alternatives. CFS combines multiple tools and strategies in pursuing its goals, including litigation and legal petitions for rule making and legal support for various sustainable agriculture and food safety constituencies, as well as public education, grassroots organizing, and media outreach. CFS publishes reports and fact sheets available at its website, including "Genetically Engineered Food: The Labeling Debate."

Center for Science in the Public Interest (CSPI)

1220 L Street NW, Suite 300, Washington, DC 20005
(202) 332-9110
e-mail: cspi@cspinet.org
website: www.cspinet.org

The Center for Science in the Public Interest (CSPI) is an organization advocating for nutrition and health, food safety, alcohol policy, and sound science. The CSPI Biotechnology Project addresses scientific concerns, government policies, and corporate practices concerning genetically engineered plants, animals, and other organisms that are released into the environment or that may end up in food. CSPI publishes several reports and reviews, including "Straight Talk on Genetically Engineered Foods: Answers to Frequently Asked Questions," available at its website.

Council for Responsible Genetics (CRG)

5 Upland Road, Suite 3, Cambridge, MA 02140
(617) 868-0870 • fax: (617) 491-5344
e-mail: crg@gene-watch.org
website: www.councilforresponsiblegenetics.org

The Council for Responsible Genetics (CRG) is a nonprofit organization dedicated to fostering public debate about the social, ethical, and environmental implications of genetic technologies. CRG works through the media and concerned citizens to distribute accurate information and represent the public interest on emerging issues in biotechnology, including genetically modified food. CRG publishes *GeneWatch*, a magazine dedicated to monitoring biotechnology's social, ethical, and environmental consequences.

Earth Open Source

2nd Floor 145–157, St John Street, London   EC1V 4PY
  United Kingdom
(44) 203 286 7156
website: www.earthopensource.org

Earth Open Source is a nonprofit organization dedicated to assuring the sustainability, security, and safety of the global food system. Earth Open Source challenges the use of pesticides, artificial fertilizer, and genetically modified organisms (GMOs) in agriculture. Earth Open Source has authored and coauthored several reports, including "GMO Myths and Truths: An Evidence-Based Examination of the Claims Made for the Safety and Efficacy of GM Crops."

Food and Agriculture Organization of the United Nations (FAO)

Viale delle Terme di Caracalla, Rome   00153
  Italy
(39) 06 57051 • fax: (39) 06 570 53152
e-mail: FAO-HQ@fao.org
website: www.fao.org

The Food and Agriculture Organization of the United Nations (FAO) is an intergovernmental organization that aims to ensure people have regular access to enough high-quality food to lead active, healthy lives. FAO aims to eliminate hunger by making agriculture more productive and sustainable, reducing rural poverty, ensuring food systems are inclusive, and protecting livelihoods from disasters. FAO publishes the annual "FAO Statistical Yearbook."

Food & Water Watch

1616 P Street NW, Suite 300, Washington, DC   20036
(202) 683-2500 • fax: (202) 683-2501
e-mail: info@fwwatch.org
website: www.foodandwaterwatch.org

Food & Water Watch works to ensure the food, water, and fish we consume are safe, accessible, and sustainably produced. Food & Water Watch promotes policies that lead to sustainable, healthy food; advocates for safe and affordable drinking water; and promotes policies that maintain the environmental quality of the ocean. Food & Water Watch publishes fact sheets and reports, such as "The Case for GE Labeling."

Friends of the Earth International (FoEI)
PO Box 19199, Amsterdam   1000 GD
   The Netherlands
(31) 20 622 1369
website: www.foei.org

Friends of the Earth International (FoEI) is a worldwide grass-roots environmental network, uniting seventy-four national member groups and some five thousand local activist groups on every continent. FoEI challenges the current model of economic and corporate globalization and aims to promote solutions that will help to create environmentally sustainable and socially just societies. FoEI has a variety of publications available at its website, including "Who Benefits from GM Crops? The Rise in Pesticide Use."

Institute of Science in Society (ISIS)
29 Tytherton Road, London   N19 4PZ
   United Kingdom
(44) 20 1908 696101
website: www.i-sis.org.uk

The Institute of Science in Society (ISIS) is a nonprofit organization that works for social responsibility and sustainable approaches in science. ISIS aims to promote critical public understanding of science and to engage both scientists and the public in open debate and discussion, particularly on the issue of genetic modification. ISIS publishes the quarterly *Science in Society* and reports such as "Ban GMOs Now."

International Service for the Acquisition of Agri-Biotech Applications (ISAAA)
DAPO Box 7777, Metro Manila
   The Philippines

(63) 2 845-0563 • fax: (63) 49 536-7216
e-mail: seasiacenter@isaaa.org
website: www.isaaa.org

The International Service for the Acquisition of Agri-Biotech Applications (ISAAA) is a nonprofit international organization that shares the benefits of crop biotechnology with various stakeholders, particularly resource-poor farmers in developing countries. ISAAA has a global knowledge-sharing network and partners for the transfer and delivery of proprietary biotechnology applications. ISAAA publishes the weekly *Crop Biotech Update* and the annual *Global Status of Commercialized Biotech/GM Crops*.

Navdanya

A-60, Hauz Khas, New Delhi   110 016
   India
(91) 11-26968077 • fax: (91) 11-26856795
e-mail: navdanya@gmail.com
website: www.navdanya.org

Navdanya aims to protect nature and people's rights to knowledge, biodiversity, water, and food. Navdanya works to keep seeds, biodiversity, and traditional knowledge in people's hands and opposes genetically modified crops. Navdanya publishes numerous reports and handbooks, including "No GM Crops and Food."

Union of Concerned Scientists (UCS)

2 Brattle Square, Cambridge, MA   02138-3780
(617) 547-5552 • fax: (617) 864-9405
website: www.ucsusa.org

The Union of Concerned Scientists (UCS) is a science-based nonprofit organization that works for a healthy environment and a safer world. UCS combines independent scientific research and citizen action to secure responsible changes in government policy, corporate practices, and consumer choices, including calling for more independent research on genetic engineering. UCS publishes numerous reports, including "Failure to Yield: Evaluating the Performance of Genetically Engineered Crops."

US Food and Drug Administration (FDA)
10903 New Hampshire Avenue, Silver Spring, MD   20993
(888) 463-6332
website: www.fda.gov

The Food and Drug Administration (FDA) is an agency within the US Department of Health and Human Services. The FDA is responsible for protecting public health by assuring food and drug safety, including the safety of genetically modified food. The FDA's website contains a variety of information on FDA regulation, including its statement on genetically modified plants, "Statement of Policy: Foods Derived from New Plant Varieties."

World Health Organization (WHO)
Avenue Appia 20, Geneva 27
   Switzerland
(41) 22 791-2111
website: www.who.int

The World Health Organization (WHO) is responsible for providing leadership on global health matters within the United Nations system. WHO works to shape the health research agenda, set norms and standards, articulate evidence-based policy options, provide technical support to countries, and monitor and assess health trends. WHO has numerous publications, including several on the issue of biotechnology, such as "20 Questions on Genetically Modified Foods."

Bibliography of Books

Michael Baram and Mathilde Bourrier, eds. *Governing Risk in GM Agriculture.* New York: Cambridge University Press, 2011.

Yves Bertheau, ed. *Genetically Modified and Non-Genetically Modified Food Supply Chains: Co-Existence and Traceability.* Chichester, West Sussex, United Kingdom: Wiley-Blackwell, 2012.

Mariano Bizzarri *The New Alchemists: The Risks of Genetic Modification.* Southampton, United Kingdom: WIT Press, 2012.

Luc Bodiguel and Michael Cardwell *The Regulation of Genetically Modified Organisms: Comparative Approaches.* New York: Oxford University Press, 2010.

Conrad G. Brunk and Harold G. Coward, eds. *Acceptable Genes?: Religious Traditions and Genetically Modified Foods.* Albany, NY: SUNY Press, 2009.

Luis G. Torres Bustillos and Ines Garcia Peña *Biotechnology: Health, Food, Energy, and Environment Applications.* New York: Nova Science Publishers Inc., 2013.

Colin A. Carter, GianCarlo Moschini, and Ian Sheldon, eds. *Genetically Modified Food and Global Welfare.* Bingley, England: Emerald Group Publishing Limited, 2011.

José Falck-Zepeda, Guillaume Gruère, and Idah Sithole-Niang, eds.
Genetically Modified Crops in Africa: Economic and Policy Lessons from Countries South of the Sahara. Washington, DC: International Food Policy Research Institute, 2013.

Natalie Ferry and Angharad M.R. Gatehouse, eds.
Environmental Impact of Genetically Modified Crops. Wallingford, United Kingdom: CABI, 2009.

Neal D. Fortin
Food Regulation: Law, Science, Policy, and Practice. Hoboken, NJ: Wiley & Sons, 2009.

Dennis R. Heldman, Matthew B. Wheeler, and Dallas G. Hoover, eds.
Encyclopedia of Biotechnology in Agriculture and Food. Boca Raton, FL: CRC Press, 2011.

Norma Heredia, Irene Wesley, and Santos García
Microbiologically Safe Foods. Hoboken, NJ: Wiley & Sons, 2009.

Beiquan Mou and Ralph Scorza, eds.
Transgenic Horticultural Crops: Challenges and Opportunities. Boca Raton, FL: CRC Press, 2011.

Marion Nestle
Safe Food: The Politics of Food Safety. Berkeley: University of California Press, 2010.

Aihwa Ong and Nancy N. Chen, eds.
Asian Biotech: Ethics and Communities of Fate. Durham, North Carolina: Duke University Press, 2010.

Robert Paarlberg — *Food Politics: What Everyone Needs to Know*. New York: Oxford University Press, 2010.

Mark A. Pollack and Gregory C. Shaffer — *When Cooperation Fails: The International Law and Politics of Genetically Modified Foods*. New York: Oxford University Press, 2009.

Jill Richardson — *Recipe for America: Why Our Food System Is Broken and What We Can Do to Fix It*. Brooklyn, NY: Ig Pub, 2009.

Marie-Monique Robin — *The World According to Monsanto: Pollution, Corruption, and the Control of Our Food Supply*. New York: New Press, 2010.

Michael Specter — *Denialism: How Irrational Thinking Hinders Scientific Progress, Harms the Planet, and Threatens Our Lives*. New York: Penguin Press, 2009.

Spencer S. Stober and Donna Yarri — *God, Science, and Designer Genes: An Exploration of Emerging Genetic Technologies*. Santa Barbara, CA: Praeger, 2009.

Linda Tagliaferro — *Genetic Engineering: Modern Progress or Future Peril?* Minneapolis, MN: Twenty-First Century Books, 2010.

Index

Geographic headings and page numbers in **boldface** refer to viewpoints about that country or region.

I